T0159933

DEVELOPMENTAL
STAGES
OF
Love
- The Original Theory

IRH PRESS

BOOKS

IRH PRESS

New York

ISBN 13: 978-1-942125-94-5
ISBN 10: 1-942125-94-1

Printed in Canada

First Edition

DEVELOPMENTAL STAGES OF

Love

- *The Original Theory*

PHILOSOPHY OF LOVE IN MY YOUTH

RYUHO OKAWA

IRH PRESS

Contents

CHAPTER TWO

Love and Life

CHAPTER THREE
Love and Human Beings

CHAPTER FOUR

Love and My Mission

CHAPTER FIVE

Love and the Spirit World

CHAPTER SIX

Love and the Philosophy of Happiness

Preface

The essays I wrote between the age of about 25 and 28 happened to be found. They are short papers that I wrote in my spare time when I worked for a trading house. The secretaries of our Religious Affairs Headquarters and the staff of the Editorial Division worked together to compile them into this book.

As I read the manuscript, I could not hold back my tears from welling up; the days of struggle in my youth flooded back to me.

It was not only poetry that I was writing.

I was also striving hard to crystallize my first basic philosophies in preparation for the day I would stand as a religious leader. The memories of my unknown days came back to me.

I did not spend the six years after I attained Great Enlightenment in 1981 idly. No one knows about the hours of struggle I spent to develop responsible philosophies.

As immature as it may be, this book is a precious piece preceding *The Laws of the Sun*.

At around the same time, I was preparing the early collection of messages from various spirits, but this book reveals my own basic thoughts and their original theory. In this sense, this book is like a treasure.

I hope you will appreciate each and every word to deepen your understanding of them.

Ryuho Okawa
Master & CEO of Happy Science Group
September 19, 2021

Prologue

The Monism of Love

October 11, 1982, in New York

We live in a world where only love exists. The emotions of hatred, jealousy, and anger do not stand against love. Much less, they have no power to challenge this world where only love exists.

Hatred is born from misunderstanding; jealousy from a lack of love. Anger is a form of foolish self-love or ailing self-love that comes from the desire to protect oneself.

If we realize that this world is the world of monism of love and know that the sun is brightly shining high up in the sky, unceasingly shedding its light even on cloudy days and rainy days, then our hearts will always be filled with happiness.

If we can believe that we are living in a world where only love exists, we can surely live for love and die for love.

If you can truly live for love and truly die for love, then, O humans, who else will you be but a winner of life?

O, we are indeed living in a world of Love only, of Light only.

The Development of Love and the Path of Self-Establishment

August 19

By "the theory of the developmental stages of love" I mean "the developmental stages of *love that gives*." However, this "love that gives" does not mean you should abandon yourself and serve others. Love that disregards oneself to let others live may appear like a holy love at a glance, but self-sacrifice is not love. At the basis of love is the feeling of holy oneness of the self and others, and the oneness of the self and others is based on the premise that you are a great being who you can love yourself and not someone to be rid of.

In other words, "love that gives" is the love that is filling and overflowing from a vessel, which is you.

I first want to be a great being who I can love myself. And I want my self-establishment and self-development to be, at the same time, the development of love for other people.

Self-Love → Self-Trust → Developmental Stages of Love.

CHAPTER ONE

Short Philosophical Essays on the Developmental Stages of Love

The Developmental Stages of Love

Views on life based on the monism of love

There are many works that talk about love. And myriads of people probably want to know what love truly means. This is because human beings are conditioned by love, and not a single day in our lives passes by without us thinking about love.

People are born primarily conditioned by the love of their fathers and mothers. They grow up nourished by the love of their fathers and mothers. During childhood, they come to know the love of their teachers and friends. During adolescence, they turn into adults under the condition that they experience love for someone of the opposite sex. As they reach the age of maturity, they learn to love not only their spouses and children but also their neighbors. In their middle ages, their love for society and the nation starts ripening. And in their twilight years, they turn to the love for God and love from God as they deeply reflect on their lives.

In this way, human life is a life of coming into contact with various kinds of love, and these memories of love fill the diaries of our minds with records of how we loved and were loved by others or how we did not love and were not loved by others.

All work and activities in life are the fruits of either love for others or love for the self. And whether you led a happy life is determined by whether you were blessed with encounters with love.

From this, we can say that love conditions not only human existence but also a trace of human existence or the process of one's life. It also conditions the value of happiness, which is the ultimate outcome of one's life. In this sense, one's view of life from the monism of love must also be affirmed.

If we see life through the monism of love, we should be allowed to value love as our life's goal and see encounters with various kinds of love as a measure of our growth as human beings.

In the following section, I would like to define love that is described in various ways as stages of development, not as different kinds, and discuss the hypothesis that there are different stages of human growth in parallel to the developmental stages of love.

The theory of the developmental stages of love

The first stage of love, I believe, is "fundamental love." Fundamental love arises out of a sense of equality; it is love for those who are living with you now or kindness for your contemporaries. When you are told to love others in general, it refers to this fundamental love.

Fundamental love is the love that gives, the love that keeps giving, and the love that does not expect any return. In other words, the "love" I am talking about here is altruistic love, and I regard love for oneself—or self-love—as a stage before "love." Love is love because it belongs to human beings. So self-love, which is the kind of "love" that can also be found in animals and, in a sense, plants, cannot be called true love because this love has yet to evolve into egoless love.

Love is not for oneself but for others—to know this is the first stage of love, which is fundamental love. When you are at this stage, at least you are not harming others and are living as a good citizen.

I would say that the second stage in the development of love is "nurturing love." Those who can nurture others are outstanding people. Human beings can exert nurturing love only when they have refined themselves with their talents and efforts to be able to lead others. In this sense, we can say that "nurturing love" is a more advanced state of love than "fundamental love."

This nurturing love is the love of a leader, the love of those who stand in a position of guiding others. Its power, influence, and depth of insight into human beings surpass fundamental love, which is something that each individual experiences in the course of their life. Whereas fundamental love can be said to belong to "personal love," this nurturing love can more or less be called "public love." That is why all those who practice nurturing love are commonly contributing to the betterment of society, be they excellent politicians, great businessmen, outstanding artists, or scholars who act as opinion leaders.

However, even this wonderful nurturing love has its limits. People at the stage of nurturing love are, in general, highly talented; however, ironically, shortcomings specific to talented people will restrict this love. That is because the love that tries to nurture others sometimes manifests itself as a tendency to criticize and blame other people's shortcomings. Because they are highly talented themselves, they can easily spot the faults in others and criticize them. It is just as if someone who has climbed a step higher on stone stairs is looking down at the people below. The love of someone who fiercely criticizes others with a demon face is not true love.

So, the third stage is "forgiving love." Ever since human beings were born, they have experienced being loved by others many times. They have also experienced being nurtured or guided by others every now and again. However, being forgiven by others is probably an experience they may have had only a few times, or just once, in their lifetimes.

Nurturing others is possible if we have talent. However, forgiving others is hard to practice for us ordinary people who are yet to have the power of virtue or generosity beyond talent. O blessed are those who have forgiving love! Those with a big enough caliber to forgive others are treasures in the world of human beings.

This "forgiving love" can be found mainly among philosophers, religious professionals, and educators. Those who know themselves, know others and know the secrets of the world cannot help but be tolerant of others. Those who have ascended the throne of forgiving love can even embrace those with many faults by the power of forgiveness, just like how an adult watches over the mistakes of their children.

However, even this forgiving love is not perfect. That is because the heart of forgiving others contains the willingness to forgive others after acknowledging their evil as evil. As long as you are caught up in the dualism of good and evil and are approaching good people with fundamental love and evil people with forgiving love, I must say you have yet to know the essence of the *idea* of love.

The acts of "loving," "nurturing," and "forgiving" are different expressions of love, and they do not represent love itself. Love is not an act; it is something inherent, a reality, and a real entity.

Then, as the final stage of the development of love, I would like to advocate "love incarnate."

Looking back on your life, you must have met someone whom you felt, "Oh, I'm so glad I had the opportunity of meeting such a wonderful person.

My life changed after I met that person." Or have you, yourself, ever been appreciated and told, "I'm glad to have met such a wonderful person like you"?

Love incarnate is not the sort of love found in one's thinking, speaking, or acting. It is love in the sense that a person's very existence in this world is love for us all. When the person passes by our lives, the candle of love is lit in our hearts—such a person is the embodiment of love incarnate. To put it another way, love incarnate dwells in great character; it is the power of influence that gushes out from noble character, which will surely inspire people.

The very existence of such a person inspires people and influences the world. Anyone can become a wonderful person who embodies love incarnate on a small scale. But without a doubt, at the ultimate level of love incarnate are saints and great figures. The very fact that such people lived at a particular time is the love for us all. Their very existences are love itself. They themselves are love, and they exist as if love exists. They have the power to make people feel the presence of something holy. This is the level that love will ultimately reach.

In this way, love progresses from "fundamental love" to "nurturing love" and then to "forgiving love"—the stages of love that are expressed through actions—and it finally reaches "love incarnate." This is my theory of the developmental stages of love.

Moments of Love and the Presence of Love

Love and recognition

Love can neither be seen nor touched. However, no one can deny the existence of love. It is just like how people believe in the existence of wind but cannot capture it and say, "This is wind." When the wind blows, we feel its presence; love, too, can only be recognized when it passes through our hearts. It cannot be taken out in a stationary state and shown to us by saying, "This is love."

Words themselves are not love. Actions themselves are not love, either. The presence of love cannot be proven by words or actions. Love is felt when it is in motion. A gentle gaze is not love itself; it is a moment for us to feel love. Kind deeds are not love itself; they are moments of love. Thoughtful words are not love itself; they, too, are moments of love. Then, are thoughts of love, or loving thoughts, love itself? They are very akin to love. But love is not a thought, either: for example, love is not present when you are thinking about love sitting alone in an isolation cell.

Love exists between people. Love exists in the interactions between people. Love exists as people live together. And love itself is felt through words, actions, and thoughts. It is a sense of presence. Most of the time, it remains as a sense of presence because people need to go through many trials of love before they can recognize that love is a real entity. As a matter of fact, I believe not even one in ten thousand people perceives love as a real entity.

Indeed, you cannot come to perceive love as a real entity unless you actually experience a highly contemplative life.

But people can feel the presence of love through various moments of love. And through sensing the presence of love, they eventually come to realize that love is a real entity.

The stages in recognizing love

Thus, there are several stages for people to walk on the path to love or on the path to supreme love.

The first is the primitive stage of love. This stage involves admiration, passion, interest, curiosity, and attraction toward the opposite sex. At this stage, people are still emitting immature thoughts to others, but in many cases, they misunderstand such thoughts for love. However, it is between people that love exists, not in one-sided feelings. In this sense, I call this the primitive stage of love.

The second stage is where people believe the moment of love to be love itself. Kind words expressed to others, kind words received from others, an act of kindness, offering a service, a smile, a thank-you letter, or consideration for your loved one—these certainly remind us of love, and in some cases, they may be described as love. But these are just moments, not love itself.

For example, donating to people in need or raising funds for the less fortunate is a good deed originating out of love. However, good deeds themselves are not love itself, even though they are moments to attain love.

The third stage is where people can feel the presence of love through the moments of love. Take the example of two lovers: the second stage is where they are so anxious that they have to constantly confirm their partner's love through words, whereas in the third stage, they enjoy just being together or their happiness grows just by being together. Even if they are apart, they feel like they are connected through a large invisible pipe or they can immediately understand what the other is thinking, as if by telepathy. At such times, they certainly feel the presence of something invisible.

In terms of the previous example of donating to the less fortunate, the second stage is where you make a donation because you think it is a good thing to do. The third stage is where you make a donation because you feel deeply blessed for luckily being in a position to do so and feel a natural sense of oneness with those at the receiving end welling up from within. At such times, you can certainly feel the presence of love through the moment of making a donation.

The fourth stage is where you can recognize love as a real entity. At this stage, you can see love. You can clearly see the love that dwells in people's hearts and the magnetic field of the energy of love working between people. You do not feel the presence of love through the kind words of others; rather, you feel that the kind words were given to you as a result of the working of love as a real entity.

It may not be easy to recognize love as a real entity. However, if it did not exist, why would people believe in love, work hard for it, and be weary when they fail to get it?

I think the higher people climb the path to supreme love, the more convinced they can be of the fact that love is a real entity. And the stronger their conviction that love is a real entity is, the closer they will be to the essence of happiness.

CHAPTER TWO

Love and Life

He Who Does Not Love
Does Not Know God

December 26, 1982, in New York

"He who does not love does not know God." These are words by a Japanese business leader Reisuke Ishida, who was active about a generation ago, and also words from the Bible.

These are not words of warning to those who do not believe in God. Rather, they are a warning to those who think they are living with faith in God. When our love for others runs dry, we no longer believe in God.

Let us be cautious with ourselves. Let us always check to see if our hearts are full of love for others. If there is no love in our hearts, we no longer know God.

"He who does not love does not know God."

Be Strict with Yourself

December 26, 1982, in New York

Nearly 2,000 years ago, there was a great emperor in Rome called Marcus Aurelius. In his work titled *Meditations*, he wrote, "I awake to do the work of a man." Aurelius, who was very strict with himself, woke up every morning telling himself these words.

Day after day, on winter mornings, I give in to the sweet temptation of sleeping in under warm blankets, and today I live another day regretting that I foolishly wasted time. Wasn't I born into this world to achieve something? Am I not alive to accomplish something? Yet I remain passive in a sweet morning slumber. How can I possibly accomplish the work of a man in this way?

Aurelius lived a life of being strict on himself and tolerant of others. He wanted less for himself and gave more to others. Aurelius lamented not his lack of talent but his lack of virtue. He asked himself why he did not exert his virtues of purity, unselfishness, modesty, little desire for pleasure, seriousness, freedom, simplicity, and kindness instead of bemoaning his lack of talent. Aurelius valued being taught by others rather than teaching others, despite his position as emperor.

This philosopher-emperor wrote down each of the things he learned from various people he met and compiled them into *Meditations*. O people, we too must learn from his humility and strict attitude toward himself.

The Mind Is a Mirror

November 19, 1983

Being born as a human, it is difficult to live life without committing any sins. But are human beings never given a chance to be forgiven once they commit a sin or break moral rules?

I think the human mind is like a clear mirror that is essentially unclouded and unstained. Mirrors are not always shining brightly. Sometimes they get dirty, and sometimes they get cloudy; that is when they become unable to reflect a person's figure. However, a mirror is a mirror because no matter how dirty or cloudy it gets, once the dirt and cloudiness are removed, the beautiful surface emitting its original, pure light will be revealed again.

Isn't a person's life also like a mirror? O you pitiful being, a human being who lives while continuously committing sins, your sin is not something that cannot be undone. Remember that your mind is a beautiful mirror. Wipe away your sins and defilements. For the Will of God is always shining in the human mind, like a beautiful mirror.

A Dialectic of Romantic Love

July 21, 1984

Some people may mutter that life is dull and uninteresting. Twenty-four hours a day and 365 days a year will come and go in a cycle, bringing human beings closer to death. Certainly, it is rare for people to lead a life full of ups and downs. Unlike in novels, even if someone is regarded to have had a dramatic life, those days were most probably an accumulation of quite ordinary days to that person.

However, just as there is spring as a season, God has given human life a season of adolescence. To those in the middle of this season, adolescence may feel like those thunderstorm days or the depressing sky of the rainy season, but from the perspective of a third person, it looks like a beautiful summer day with clear blue skies.

Keeping a Rein on Your Tongue

August 1, 1984

Keeping a rein on your tongue is impossible without going through a great deal of training. I myself can hardly say I am sufficiently keeping a rein on my tongue yet.

Some people complain that bad words just slip out against their will. Others believe they are good-hearted despite their sharp tongues. But they are not true. The mouth is not another creature that acts on its own. A bad mouth comes out because of a bad heart. Bad words come out because you have a bad heart. So first correct the distorted part of your mind. Look squarely at when and under which circumstances you utter bad words to others.

I used to think that I had a sharp tongue because I inherited it from my mother. And I believed that it was something I could never control. However, I also realized that I could more or less hold back bad words on the day I made up my mind not to speak bad words. If having a sharp tongue was hereditary, it would be extremely difficult to correct it through effort. Indeed, a sharp tongue is a matter of habit rather than heredity. If you can make enough efforts to break the power of this bad habit, then you will also be able to keep a rein on your tongue.

I said that bad words come out because you have a bad heart. The bad side of your heart is, after all, the part that has been hurt. Those with a wound in their hearts will unexpectedly hurt the hearts of others. And often the wound in your mind is actually your inferiority complex. Those with an inferiority complex delude themselves while defiling others using bad words. We want to detest and abandon the bad habit of hurting people in an attempt to just temporarily taste a sense of superiority.

The Path of Learning

August 1, 1984

How wonderful it is to be able to learn things in this world! If experience gives breadth to life, then learning gives depth.

Imagine a river, for example. Going through various life experiences is like a river running through mountains, hills, and plains and eventually expanding and flowing downstream. On the other hand, the color of the river tells its depth. People do not try to directly measure the depth of the river, but the color of the water eloquently tells how deep it is. At times, the river may appear to be deep blue, and at other times, deep green. The darkness of the blue color signifies the level of culture the person gained by deeply exploring the path of learning.

After all, the depth of your culture is the result of how much you have developed yourself.

The Path to Attaining Love

August 1, 1984

"Attaining Love"—how beautiful it sounds! The phrase is not about taking love or obtaining love but about attaining love. These words paint a beautiful image of someone who keeps on walking steadily and tirelessly with love as their life's goal. Love that you take from others will be taken away someday, and love that can be obtained will be abandoned someday.

Attaining love, or steadily walking on the path to supreme love—isn't this nothing but the best possible life?

O people, the path to attaining love is challenging and tough. No matter how high you climb, you will not be able to see the summit, and the moment you think of only yourself, you will immediately fall. It is such a severe path.

Self-Power and Other-Power

August 18, 1984

In religion, there are mainly two types of teaching—one focusing on Self-Power and the other focusing on Other-Power. There may be many different arguments over which teaching is true.

But I think Self-Power and Other-Power are like two wheels of a car for religion; the car will not move forward if one of them is missing.

To use a metaphor, praying, wishing, and asking for help from Other-Power is the same as expecting a ladder to come down from heaven. Prayers will always be heard. A ladder will always come down from heaven.

However, you can only climb the ladder step by step through Self-Power. God does not go so far as to bind human beings with a rope and pull them up to heaven. It is up to each person's own free will to decide whether to climb the ladder or not or how to climb it.

O humans, pray. Through prayer, find the ladder from heaven. Only then will you fully enjoy the Self-Power that gets you out of pain.

The Best Possible Life

July 22, 1984

Everyone wishes to live the best possible life. However, very few people can declare what the best life is. The approach that has relatively fewer mistakes is probably to trace back the footsteps of great figures of the past and find out their common traits or the fundamental principles.

Like Carl Hilty, if you define happiness as God's companionship, then perhaps the best life for you would be to live while feeling God close to you.

St. Bernard of Clairvaux categorized the love for God into four stages: 1) loving yourself for your own sake, 2) loving others in the name of God, 3) loving God for the sake of God, and 4) loving yourself only for the sake of God. If you understand that love is something that develops like this, you will be able to say you have lived the best life when you have fully used your life as a tool of God's love.

Miss Helen Keller wrote, "Unless, like the lily, we can rise pure and strong above sordid surroundings, we would probably be moral weaklings in any situation. Unless we can help the world where we are, we could not help it if we were somewhere else. The most important question is not the sort of environment we have, but the kind of thoughts we think every day, the kind of ideals we are following," and "Only by striving for what is beyond us do we win expansion and joy" (from Helen Keller's *My Religion*). According to her ideas, the best life would be to overcome a difficult environment and become a light for the world through efforts.

Then, how would I describe the best life for me? From any standpoint, I cannot say that the best life is for human beings to go through trial and error as they live based on the belief that they were materialistically born by chance. That is because life without insight into the true nature of human beings is equal to nothing. Human beings do not happen to be living by chance. We are allowed to live. We are kept alive by a great, invisible force. All things live in a world created by this great, invisible power.

For me, the first step to the best possible life is to have a view that human beings are being allowed to live in this world by a great power. It is precisely because you think you are alone and are living by chance, through trial and error, that your life becomes dark, sad, and full of suffering. It is precisely because you only think of your own good that your life becomes fruitless. To put it another way, the first step to the best possible life is to have a view that God allows all beings to live.

Then, what is the second step to the best possible life? I believe it is to be aware of love, to know love, and to live love. The road of life without love is a road in the desert. But love is an oasis, a green shade, and a brief, cool breeze. Being aware of the presence of such love, knowing the presence of such love, giving birth to such love through your own efforts, and becoming such an oasis, green shade, and brief, cool breeze yourself for others—there must have been not a single great figure in history who lived without such an idea. Can the life of a person who searches for an oasis just to quench his thirst, without any thought of becoming an oasis for others, ever be called the best life? That is why I believe that encountering love is the second step to the best possible life.

So what would be the third step to the best possible life? I think it is to make efforts. The life of a person who lives by the creed, "Making efforts is happiness, and happiness is making efforts," is like a straight road shining in the sun after the rain. In contrast, some people may advocate the idea of "making no conscious effort and taking things as they come." But while this idea can offer an opportunity to free human beings from attachment and lead them to enlightenment, I feel it is missing the mission of human beings being born into this world to fulfill.

The road of life is the road of endeavor. People are inspired when they see the back of someone walking up the slope of effort. Your life will be too sad if you leave this world without leaving behind a good influence on others and the young people to come. If you lived the best life, you will definitely leave behind something that is more than what can be seen for others, just as water flows from a higher place to a lower place.

The fourth step to the best possible life is to awaken to spirituality. Those who are aware of their spiritual nature and can see the world from a spiritual perspective are already living extraordinary lives. You must pass through a gate to awaken to spirituality— the gate of the dualism of good and evil. You cannot awaken to and grasp your spiritual nature without experiencing conversion, in the Christian context, or self-reflection, in the Buddhist context. When you pass through this gate of good and evil, you develop a considerably acute sense of right and wrong. And your regret for what you did wrong in the past will lead you to repent, convert your mind, or reflect on yourself in light of the Eightfold Path. When you have cleared the clouds over your mind, everything in the world will look like they are shining as if the sun is brightly shining on them.

At that time, you will come to know one theorem—the idea that love is a higher concept than good and evil. If we take love as a wave, good is the crest of the wave and evil is the trough. Crests and troughs come and go in many patterns to produce a wave of love. There is no good without evil and no evil without good. And beyond the shores of good and evil, human beings will attain love. Love is at the basis of spirituality.

To get a glimpse of what lies at the depths of this world, human beings must insert a key called love and push the door open. The world seen through the light of spirituality is a world full of joy, happiness, and beauty. There is no good or evil in this world; people are innocently having fun.

There are no worries or sufferings; look, the spring warmth is in the air. People believe in one another on the grounds that everyone believes in God.

In that world, there are only two criteria to measure a person's greatness. One is how deeply you have understood the true nature of human beings and, eventually, the true nature of God. The other is how widely you have loved people. In other words, it is the grandness of your heart to love others. Such people are respected, and everyone is striving to be such a person in this world.

Unless we awaken to our spirituality and come to see such kind of world in this present world, we cannot say we are fully living our lives in the truest sense.

Thus, we can say that the fourth and final step to the best possible life is to awaken to spirituality.

CHAPTER THREE

Love and Human Beings

Love and Lust

May 3, 1984

People all have big dreams when they are young. The greatest dream of all would be to serve the people of the world and devote themselves to building a better society.

I was no exception. When I was 11 years old, I read the biography of Albert Schweitzer and was deeply inspired by his lofty ideals and pure life. Schweitzer decided to focus on himself until the age of 30 and dedicate the rest of his life to other people, and he actually devoted himself to learning, such as music and medicine, until he was 30. Especially this way of life of Schweitzer, in no small way, influenced my life over the 10 and some odd years since then.

However, the teens and twenties are the age of flourishing. Flowers should be enjoyed when they are in bloom; otherwise, they will sadly wither away. The days of youth are too sweet and too tempting to complete the groundwork for serving other people. And everyone must go through life's trials of love and lust during this period.

During the days of adolescence, members of the opposite sex look attractive, and it is difficult to say whether your feelings toward someone are love or lust. Only when your days of adolescence have passed do you gradually recognize these feelings, but not very clearly. Young people call them romantic love, but romantic love is like a pendulum that swings between love and lust. It appears that the second half of a person's life depends on where this pendulum named romantic love stops—at love or at lust.

When it comes to choosing between love and lust, I believe young people should choose love. No matter how sweet lust may seem, at its base is only self-satisfying egoism, with no consideration, kindness, or respect for the other person and no aspiration for improvement. Love is essentially the respect for other people's true nature hidden within them. Love is the mutual resonance of divine nature that lies in yourself as well as in other people. Love aims at the mutual improvement of the self and others—others and the self. Is there an aspiration for improvement in lust? The only things you can find there are passing pleasure and eternal emptiness.

"Born and reborn again and again, we are ignorant at the beginnings of birth; dying again and again and yet again, we are nescient at the ending of death" (Kukai[1]). We are all born alone and die alone. That is our life. If we are to make a flower bloom during the short period of adolescence, we should aim to make bloom, not an artificial flower called lust but, a living flower called love.

[Memo]
- About the stages of recognition
- Ultimate truth, ultimate love, ultimate holiness
- About an affectionate character
- Moment of happiness

Love and Virginity

August 26 / September 2, 1984

When speaking of love, if we overlook the issue of sexuality, then half of the people's worries concerning love will forever be left unresolved. When it comes to the issue of how love between men and women should be in their adolescence, in particular, it is almost impossible for anyone to speak with authority in today's society, where religion has little influence. So I would like to talk about the love and virginity of men and women who are yet to get married.

Is physical virginity necessary for a man and a woman before marriage? The history of humankind suggests that the majority's view has been that physical virginity is necessary. This is in line with the Confucian moral that states, "After the age of seven, boys and girls should not sit together," and with the philosophies of Christianity and Buddhism.

In contrast, in the context of Christian countries, for example, Thomas Hardy wrote the novel *Tess of the d'Urbervilles*. In it, he depicts how an innocent girl, Tess, unwillingly loses her virginity and confesses it to her fiancé, which leads to her downfall. Hardy posed the question, "If God should exist, how could He be so merciless?" This is atheism that arises from the issue of virginity. André Gide of France wrote *Strait Is the Gate*, which depicts in detail how Alissa's and Jérôme's platonic love of a Christian touch—overly Christian touch—leads to a tragedy. In Japan, Yoichi Nakagawa wrote the novel *A Moonflower in Heaven*. It depicts the sad story of a man who devotes his life to a love that is too pure.

I think extreme Puritanism is apt to view sex as a sin; it does not bring about the boundless fruit of love. Even today, it is not rare to hear of the misfortune of a pious Catholic woman who missed her chance to get married because she was too pure.

When considering the issue of the virginity of men and women in this present age, we must take into account the following points: First, now that birth control methods have developed, losing one's virginity does not immediately lead to pregnancy. Second, men and women are getting married at a later age because they pursue higher education and also because of their economic condition. As a result, there is almost a 10-year difference between their age of biological or sexual maturity and their age of marriage. The first point indicates the possibility of sex becoming a sport or entertainment. The second point indicates how difficult it is for average people to live in sexual abstinence for 10 years unless they have a strong motive to do so.

From the above, I have come to believe that some kind of spiritual value must be created to demand the virginity of unmarried men and women.

I think one such spiritual value is "admiration." Because you are unsatisfied, your admiration for the unknown becomes stronger. This admiration then becomes the driving force for you to endlessly pursue something beautiful.

If I were to refer to my own admiration, I recall, with utmost nostalgia, my university days—the period between the age of 19 and 24, when I was most sensitive to and had the most yearning for women. There were days when I could not stop my flame of lust from burning up, and there were days when I felt depressed as if dark clouds were hanging over me. There was even a time when an embarrassing thought crossed my mind—the thought of following a beautiful woman as she passed by in front of me.

During those five years at university, I studied European political history and political philosophies and devoted myself to studying the six codes of modern Japanese law. I have a fond memory of looking up and unexpectedly spotting a bright crescent moon over the Red Gate of the University of Tokyo as I walked down the dark pathway of ginkgo trees in the Hongo campus after leaving the library late at night.

I also remember finding crimson ume (Japanese plum) subtly blooming on a snowy day as I was taking a stroll in Umegaoka, near my lodging and sending a single ume flower to a woman I admired in an envelope enclosed with a poem I wrote. By the way, I was actually too shy to even speak to her.

Looking back, I was too simple and too pure during my university days. For five years, I studied very hard while harboring a secret yearning for a woman in a corner of my heart and just admiring from afar the loved one I had yet to meet or my future wife. I never joined drinking binges, played mahjong, or dated a woman; only my ideals and admiration far off in the distance occupied my mind.

Considering my own university days, I feel sorry for the young people who have already engaged in sexual relations in their teens and can only see the beauty and ugliness of the opposite sex through physical desire. Admiration for the opposite sex will eventually fade with age. However, it seems to me that how long we have kept this feeling of admiration will greatly influence the rest of our lives.

Simply put, there are two types of people—one of spirit and the other of flesh—and the more we get rid of materialistic aspects, the more we grow into spiritual people. Looking at someone of the opposite sex with the feeling of admiration is equal to discovering beauty in its most perfect form.

The second spiritual value that demands the virginity of unmarried men and women is "purity." Jesus said in the Sermon on the Mount: "Blessed are the pure in heart, for they shall see God." This holy man taught us the way to see God: "being pure in heart." This is evident in the lives of Truth seekers, religious leaders, and philosophers of the past.

To be pure in the mind means to have a clear lens of the mind. If your lens of the mind is crystal clear, you will come to see God, the laws of the universe, and the workings of love. For those seeking such a supreme value, stubbornly sticking to preserving their virginity for a certain period of time is quite important.

I have talked about the importance of virginity. But nowadays, the majority of men and women probably lose their virginity before they get married. If we were to apply the idea that human beings are born sinful, as taught by some Christians, then a mass of sinners is living in this world, and hell would be quite busy due to overpopulation.

I think extreme demands on virginity will make us narrow-minded and strict on others, causing us to see everyone around us as sinful people.

However, human beings are by no means children of sin. We are not children of sin but children of love. Each one of us was not born sinful, bearing a cross, but born as children of love to manifest love in this world. If God is love, we too must be love. And we are supposed to go on a journey of life as "love incarnate."

To use a metaphor, we who are "children of love" are like diamonds in the rough. With a little polishing, you will become an embodiment of "fundamental love," and with good polishing, you will become an embodiment of "nurturing love." By polishing yourself further, you will reach the stage of "forgiving love." And when you become like the most beautifully polished diamond, you have developed the character as "love incarnate," making others feel the presence of love itself, and your very presence becomes love for us all.

If we consider what it means to lose one's virginity based on the idea that human beings are children of love, we will come to understand that the mere fact that a person has lost their virginity does not mean that the person has lost their value as a human being. No matter how much filth, dirt, or dust covers it, a diamond is still a diamond; it never loses its value. The main thing to remember is that if you, yourself, are not aware of your own value as a diamond, the diamond will only be thrown away, by you as well as by others, as a mere clump of earth.

After all, I think it is a matter of whether you can grow into a big-hearted person who can forgive others through the experience of losing your virginity or start living negatively after losing it.

When thinking about marriage, we must say it is the start of a new life. Love should start with trust, not with doubt. Preserving virginity will lead to the case where love starts with trust. Your having lost virginity will lead you to start married life with a handicap, but the point is whether you can build a trusting relationship that transcends doubt.

One thing we should not forget is that sex is a moment that leads to romantic love, and romantic love is the biggest moment to attain love. When sex is misused, it degenerates into lust and cannot lead us to romantic love. We need to reconsider sex and virginity also from the perspective that they are moments to attain supreme love.

Love and Its Enemies

August 4/5, 1984

I have talked a lot about love. However, to truly know the path to attaining love, we must not neglect to explore the obstacles of love or the issue of love and its enemies. I say this because the light seems to shine even more brightly when darkness is recognized. So the true nature of love will become more and more apparent as we recognize the obstacles of love.

The enemies of love that I talk about here do not necessarily stand against love; rather, they come into the laboratory of love called life more than once, and with one misstep, they will lead us astray from the path to supreme love.

(1) Love and stoicism

Living stoically, or going through an abstinent period in some way, seems to be essential; it offers moments to attain love. This is because, first, love is spiritual and, second, love is altruistic.

First, with regard to the fact that love is spiritual, stoicism is an effective moment to lead to love because at the center of stoicism lies the restraint of material desires to attain spiritual heights. It is true that we cannot transcend into the spiritual realm if we are attached to worldly or material things. We cannot come to see the true nature of love unless we cut off worldly things in some respect.

Second, although love is altruistic, if we are left as we are after being born and raised, we will not find altruistic thoughts welling up like an inexhaustible fountain. It is rather the selfish thoughts that naturally well up until we become aware of the true nature of our minds. In other words, at the initial stage toward love, we need to make a conscious effort to restrain selfish thoughts and turn them into altruistic thoughts. Stoicism offers a good training ground for this.

As described above, stoicism urges us to think about something spiritual and shift our minds to altruistic thoughts. However, it can also become an enemy of love. Although stoicism can be a moment to lead to love, if you set stoicism as the purpose of life, your love will wither and die.

This is because, first of all, those who have practiced stoicism for a long time tend to give off a particular sense of rejection, even though love includes tolerance for others in its nature. Because they are so strict about their own ways of life, they become very strict to others as well and grow more and more intolerant and unaccepting.

The second case in which stoicism becomes an enemy of love is when it leads you to loneliness or lofty solitude. Indeed, lofty solitude indicates that a person has attained a certain level of spiritual height, but it sometimes makes you unsociable. That is why stoicism can often become an enemy of love, whose habitat lies between people.

There is only one case in which a person in lofty solitude owing to extreme stoicism can participate in love: when the person is approved by the public and has earned the respect of many people. In this case, the person is practicing love in that his thoughts or ways of life can serve as a role model to others. His love is more like mercy than love in its original sense. If love is a horizontal light that shines between human beings, then mercy is a vertical light shining down from God, or someone close to God, on all beings.

The third case in which stoicism becomes the enemy of love is when it serves as a bridge to egoism instead of offering the moment for altruism. Originally, stoicism should work to avoid pleasure and restrain material desires in order to return to God—the original source of spirituality—and become one with the power that nurtures all beings and keeps them alive. However, when stoicism is used as a tool for you to feel that you are different from others, that you are special, that you have been consecrated by God, then it goes against the spirit of love, whose basic principle lies in the oneness of the self and others.

Therefore, you who aspire to love—you must be aware that stoicism can also be an enemy of love.

(2) Love and intellect

Now, let us think about love and intellect. Intellect undoubtedly offers an important moment for love. This is because love without intellect will deteriorate into blind love, emotional love, and sometimes even animal love. Intellect is the blade that severs right from wrong. Love is always right, and wrong love is not true love.

To take an example, let us imagine a good-natured man. He does not speak badly of others. He is very kind to others and does not hesitate to give out money and goods. When asked to do something, he even tries to do more than what he is expected to do. However, if we look into the true nature of his mind with our mind's eye, we can see that he has the desire to be thought well of by others and the cowardice of wanting to protect himself from being criticized by others. After all, a good-natured disposition is often another form of self-love. Although he may believe himself to be someone of deep love, he is actually unable to objectively see his own behavior because he lacks intellect. Sometimes, the blind love of parents toward their children can also give rise to various misfortunes owing to their lack of intellect.

So intellect serves love as a blade to sever right love from wrong love or as the third eye to guarantee objectivity.

However, sometimes intellect becomes an enemy of love. The first case is when intellect is used as the absolute measure to evaluate a person. For example, as the academic background is highly valued in our society, sometimes a particular measurement to gauge a person's intellectual level can be used to evaluate the person as a whole. People with high intellectual abilities may indeed be considered worthy of respect in terms of their usefulness to the world. However, intellect is just one aspect of human talent, and it is often in a different dimension from love, which mainly emphasizes the aspect of virtue.

Moreover, whereas intellect is often the wisdom of acknowledging differences, love is about the wisdom of acknowledging equality. In other words, love is based on the wisdom of acknowledging equality, which urges people to treat human beings equally. On the other hand, if intellect is valued for its wisdom of acknowledging differences that recognizes the different levels of human abilities, then intellect will work as a repulsive force against love. To put it simply, as your intellect develops, other people will often appear foolish or inferior to you, impeding your heart of love that essentially cares for one another.

The second case in which intellect becomes an enemy of love is when intellect is used as a tool for a selfish cause. In general, the higher your intellect, the more things you will learn, the higher the awareness you will gain, the more sensitive you will become to social injustice and social evil, and the more your mind will naturally turn toward making society a better place to live. However, if your high level of intellect is used to achieve your own personal success, wealth, or fame only, it will lead you on the path to selfishness, steering you far away from the love that is based on altruism. Selfish intellect can thus become a blade for you to build your own glory upon the dead bodies of others. That is why it is an enemy of love.

(3) Love and romantic love

Romantic love is such a sweet thing. How beautiful it is to have a period during your adolescence where you fall in love with someone of the opposite sex in a life of only 60–70 years! This alone makes me feel that life is truly wonderful.

When people think of love, they may immediately think of love for the opposite sex or romantic love. That is fine because romantic love is intended to be the biggest moment for people to attain love. Isn't it true that no matter how evil or saintly a person may be called, whether they are tall or short, fat or thin, or healthy or sick, they will equally have a longing for the opposite sex during adolescence? What a wonderful thing it is that everyone has the experience of at least falling in love with another person! If I may use the word "God," we can say that God created the two sexes—man and woman—and designed them so they will experience romantic love as a moment— the greatest moment—for all to become aware of love, know love, and live love. So we can think of romantic love as the most important thing to attain love.

However, many people have probably witnessed or experienced how romantic love deteriorates from true love. This is because romantic love also serves as a severe trial for us to attain love.

The first case in which romantic love becomes an enemy of love is when a man and a woman engage in sexual union without having something spiritual between them. Sexual union itself is a natural act for a man and a woman, so I believe the act of having sex itself is neither good nor evil in essence but is value-neutral. It can work for good or evil depending on whether it enhances happiness. It is also true that sexual activity adds color to life, promotes harmony, and becomes a source of energy.

The problem is that sexual activity has an enchanting power to confine human beings into flesh, and it can work against the power of the spirit that leads us to the heights of supreme love, to be closer to God. The physical body is merely a boat for the soul, and losing the ability to punt and becoming caught up in the flow of the stream means the person's life is at a red light.

The second case in which romantic love becomes an enemy of love is when it gives rise to different kinds of vice. If romantic love gives birth to jealousy, possessiveness, or suspicion out of overly obsessive feelings, it will become a selfish feeling that contradicts altruism, which is the essential nature of love. One philosopher clearly perceived that the opposite of love is not hatred but jealousy. After all, jealousy, possessiveness, and suspicion contradict the original mental inclination that comes with love, which is the feeling of oneness of the self and others. In this sense, the byproduct of romantic love can become an enemy of love.

(4) Love and ambition

Love can be elevated by two kinds of pure ambitions. They are both ambitions to improve yourself—one is the desire to grow toward holiness, toward supreme holiness, and the other is the desire to advance toward goodness, toward supreme goodness.

Let me first talk about the ambition to be holy. This ambition accords with one of the true natures of love, which is the desire to present yourself before the great source of spirituality. I could say that ultimate love means merging with the sacred power that is omnipresent in the universe. In other words, those who aspire to be holy and to get closer to God must naturally become a great vessel of love.

The other one is the ambition to be good, or the ambition to reach ultimate goodness. It will be completed by acts of love based on altruism.

Since ancient times, those who became saints and great figures all had these two kinds of pure ambitions. However, these two ambitions can also become enemies of love.

The reason is that, first, the seeds of self-display lie hidden even in the wish to be holy and the wish to be good. The desire for self-display rots love because self-display is focused on This Shore and not on the Other Shore.

The second reason why these two ambitions become enemies of love is that the aspiration to become a saint and the aspiration to be good can sometimes manifest themselves as hypocrisy. Hypocrisy is the death of the soul. Hypocrisy is nothing but selfishness in disguise. So it is inevitably an enemy of love.

(5) Love and "neurosis"

Being sensitive is vital for people who live in love. Those who have started walking the great path of love must have had a period of making keen analysis of their own inner world and keen observation of the inner workings of other people's minds. Without delicate attention to and care for the minds of oneself and others, love will not be complete as a form of beauty, even though it can fulfill some of its functions. That is because love is something complete.

However, if this sensitiveness goes too far to develop "neurosis," it can become a terrible enemy of love.

Here I mean "neurosis" in not strictly the medical sense. The types of "neurosis" that can become enemies of love are worries about the past and anxieties about the future—or what is known as an anxious mind in general.

In the Book of Job, the righteous man laments that all he had feared came upon him. It is not rare for people with an anxious mind to more or less experience their worries befalling them.

The first enemy is the worry about the past; it is the habit of dwelling on what has already happened. People with this mental tendency will always be worrying about something throughout their lives. We can say that they have developed a "poverty mentality" regarding happiness.

However, if we think deeply regarding the worry about the past, we will come to realize that it is the consequence of having excessive self-love and the fruit of a perfectionist, mysophobic disposition. The same can be said of some religious believers who rigidly stick to the idea that human beings are born sinful and who are binding themselves tight. When you become overly sensitive to your unhappiness only and become dull to your happiness, you cannot live for the love of others.

Let's say love is like a state of spiritual abundance or a situation in which you can lend your assistance as much as you want, then the people who are constantly worrying about the past are in spiritual debt, meaning they constantly go into debt, causing trouble for others. Merely regretting past mistakes does not help to clear this debt. The only ways to do so are to work hard in the present and bring your spiritual disposition into a positive balance. Love is born of spiritual disposition with a positive balance.

Anxiety about the future is the second enemy of love. This arises because you are too sensitive to your unhappiness about the future; it is also the fruit of self-love. We all want our future to be good. However, if we start to worry only about that, we will become less considerate of other people.

To defeat this enemy of love, or anxiety about the future, you need to see yourself from a detached perspective and understand that your life is not for yourself only and that it is a lighting apparatus that has been rented to you to illuminate the world.

(6) Love and inferiority complex

With the development of civilization, people have developed diverse types of inferiority complexes. In ancient times, people's inferiority complex was most probably focused on their physical aspects, such as having strong arms or weak arms. In modern times, in addition to such physical aspects, various mental conflicts have created many complicated complexes. I would like to discuss this inferiority complex and love.

Why do we have an inferiority complex? The most common moment is probably found in the act of comparing ourselves with others. We see the strengths and weaknesses of others and then compare them with our own strengths and weaknesses. When we feel we are inferior, this feeling becomes an inferiority complex. Or we may have an inferiority complex over what we are secretly agonizing over.

One benefit of having an inferiority complex in connection to love is that it generates a form of kindness. Those with an inferiority complex can understand the feelings of others who agonize over a similar complex. People who worry that they are not smart will feel sympathy for others who have a similar problem. Those who have suffered from poverty will have a sense of compassion toward a poor young man. Some might say, "You deserve it. You should suffer from poverty just like I did," but such people have very poor minds. Not many people in the world would say something like this. A young man who has had his heart broken repeatedly and is worried he would never be loved by women will eventually find himself in a position to comfort those who are grieving in their relationships.

Thinking about it in this way, we will come to realize that an inferiority complex can provide a basis for understanding human weakness and sadness, and it offers a moment to evoke kindness and sympathy for others. Sympathy is an emotion very akin to love.

However, in many cases, an inferiority complex seems to become an enemy of love. The first enemy is self-abasement. When people demean themselves, they will not only be unable to love others but also eventually start to reject love from others.

The second enemy is competitiveness. It is a state where you always compare yourself with others and feel uneasy unless you find yourself better than them. After all, hidden in the depths of an inferiority complex is infinite self-love.

At the end of the day, an inferiority complex comes from the awareness that you are living in the world of relativity, in the world of comparative degrees. It stems from your immaturity in that you are ignorant of the existence of absolute value— that there is the world of the original source, the world of absolute that is filled with love.

Love does much more than just heal people's inferiority complex. I think the only way to eliminate the inferiority complex is to attain love by developing stronger consideration for others, which is merit particular to the inferiority complex.

CHAPTER FOUR

Love and My Mission

The Path to the Truth

The story I am about to tell you begins in the winter of 1981. At the time, I was a fifth-year student in the Faculty of Law, the University of Tokyo (I was enrolled for an extra year so that I could take the bar exam). I had been offered a job at a major general trading company called Tomen Corporation (which was initially established off of Mitsui & Co. and has now merged with Toyota Tsusho Corporation), and I was engaged in my final studies as a student, preparing for my graduation exam to be held in February.

My lodging was located in Setagaya, Tokyo, near Higashi-Matsubara Station on the Keio Inokashira Line. I was renting a room alone on the second floor of a house owned by an old local family by the name of Funabashi. Inside the six–tatami-mat room (of about 10 square meters or 105 square feet) were four large bookshelves, all of which were filled with books. Looking back, I spent much of my student life deeply immersed in reading. I gave top priority to becoming a cultured person so that I could be an effective member of society, and because I hate losing by nature, I led my student life with books as my only asset.

One day, I went downstairs to the bathroom to wash my face. I looked at my face in the mirror and found that my eyes were glowing in a peculiar manner. If I were to describe them exactly as I saw them, my small eyes were wide open, taking on an indescribable glow. Although they did not give me a very good impression, I thought they were signs indicating that some kinds of spiritual phenomena would happen in the future. And it was not long before this became a reality.

On Endurance

October 11, 1982

No great thinker was free of slander by others. No great religious leader was free of humiliation by others.

The names of those who ridiculed Socrates have faded from history, but there is not a single person who hasn't heard of Socrates' name.

Jesus, who told people, "Love your enemies," was surrounded by a multitude of enemies. I wonder how many people believed that Jesus' words indeed came from God and that he was not talking tough.

So you, who love the Truth, do not give in. Do not think little of yourself. Be brave and endure. Jesus, who prayed as he sweated blood in the Garden of Gethsemane, must have been lonely. Moses, who wandered with hundreds of thousands of people for more than 40 years during the Exodus, must have also been lonely.

If so, endure any slander, any humiliation, and any loneliness. By enduring, our lives will develop inner light.

The Genius of Love

August 3, 1984

A genius is a person who stands firm beyond the times and yet has the power to change the times they are living in. I believe that the qualities of a genius are innate. We, the ordinary people, can hardly stand firm beyond the times even with extraordinary efforts.

Indeed, not everyone can become a genius in mathematics or physics. Not everyone can become a great thinker of the world. Not everyone will become a genius writer of novels or poetry, either. An outstanding revolutionary will only appear once in a century, and it is always during the revolutionary period in world history that great discoveries or inventions of the century are made.

However, there is a way in which every one of us can become a genius through our efforts. It is by digging up the "genius of love" buried in our hearts. Love is not something that can be created artificially. It is already given to us as an innate quality.

Everyone is guaranteed to become a genius as long as they are willing to go through the trouble of digging up what has been buried.

"Genius of Love"—what a great title it is! When the medal named "Genius of Love" is hung around your neck, you will find the following words inscribed on its back:

"This person is a genius of love because, as a result of exploring the inner self, this person has found that their very existence is love itself and has made others aware of it as well."

The Loss of Love, the Anxiety over Love— The Time When You Are Forsaken by the World

June 16/17, 1984

It is difficult to avoid experiencing various hardships in the course of our lives. The greatest sadness for those living earnestly would be that of having been forsaken by the world. Many people have probably more or less experienced the same sorrow Jeremiah felt when he was forsaken by the world. When we are forsaken by the world, our souls are deeply wounded, but this is also the time when our souls can grow greater by trying to close our wounds.

The first case in which people feel they have been forsaken by the world is when they are abandoned by someone they love. Like a baby who cries out of thirst for its mother's love, people cry bitterly at the depths of their souls when they are abandoned by their loved ones.

To love someone means to offer them something invisible that lies inside yourself. As it is said, "The universe abhors a vacuum," if you have released something invisible that lies inside yourself, you will unconsciously expect something invisible to flow into you in return. When you are abandoned by your loved one, the flow of this "something" stops, and the void that suddenly appears in your heart will fill you with a sense of emptiness.

When you are abandoned by your loved one, how should you face life? I am not writing this essay for the unsentimental, strong young people who can seek new lovers one after another. I am writing this for the vulnerable young people who weep as they watch the sunset and lament over their own weakness as they watch the sunrise.

When abandoned by a loved one, people are apt to hastily attempt to rebuild themselves. They might meet with many people to trumpet their misfortune, work too energetically, or suddenly take up something new. However, my advice is this: when you are abandoned by your loved one, keep your lips sealed like a clam and endure the days bearing a heart as heavy as lead for the time being— on one hand, to reshape your weak character that tries to trumpet your misfortune and indulge in self-pity; on the other hand, to buy time so you can fully taste the sour "lemon" your life has given you and make lemonade out of it.

When abandoned by our loved ones, we feel as if we are plunged into darkness and are rejected by the whole world. But at such times, let us think rationally. Looking back on your life, you may have had someone you secretly had feelings for, even though that person was unaware of these feelings. The same can be said of you. Although some people may deny their love for you and say bad things about you, there will always be people who like you.

When you are abandoned by the one you love, you have no choice but to wait for the time and circumstances to change and lead you in a different direction. But the answer to the way out lies in how you can deepen the understanding of yourself during that time. This is the challenge each one of you is entrusted with.

The second case when people feel forsaken by the world is when they are misunderstood and ridiculed by their own family, their friends, and the general public.

There is a saying, "How can swallows and sparrows understand the ambitions of wild swans?" Usually, the potential of an ambitious young man is nipped in the bud by the thoughtless criticisms of those around him who believe they know everything about him. What is more, this problem gets even more difficult because whether the young man is a wild swan or not is mostly determined later by the results he achieves, and it is almost impossible at the time for even the young man himself to be convinced that he is a wild swan. Even if he believes he is a wild swan, the stronger his conviction, the more he will be misunderstood or ridiculed.

I have often seen young people with burning passion and ideals be humiliated out of misunderstanding and ridicule. Alas, poor me, I have also ridiculed such a person more than once.

Take, for example, the philosopher Schopenhauer. Wasn't it his mother who pushed him down the stairs because she believed herself to be a genius and that there couldn't possibly be two geniuses in the world? Wasn't it Xanthippe, notorious for being a bad wife, who swore at Socrates and, of all things, poured a chamber pot over his head?

To people who are misunderstood and ridiculed by the world, I say: People will never know whether you are fallen behind the times or far ahead of the times. People can only see that you are just outside the framework according to the world's common sense. So listen to your inner voice. If you feel your belief is pure and just, you simply need to go on to live the way you believe. Then, people of the world will eventually start to follow you in droves.

I myself believe that a lot of geniuses have now been born in Japan, just like in ancient Greece and

Rome or like how it used to be in Britain, Germany, and France. O geniuses, endure and live through misunderstanding and ridicule. This is the price you must definitely pay to build a new era. During the times you remain obscure, work quietly and silently build up your strength. As long as you stay cheerful, the buds of hope will surely grow over the face of the earth.

The third case when people feel they have been forsaken by the world is when they feel they are standing alone on untrodden ground. It is when they come to realize they themselves have to pave their own road because there is no one to guide them; it is when they tell themselves, "There is no teacher in my life." In other words, people also feel abandoned by the world when they are at the peak of lofty solitude.

A great example of this would be Jesus Christ. I believe he, too, must have felt he had been forsaken by the world. Nonetheless, I do not think it was when he was being crucified on Golgotha that he really felt he was abandoned by the world. I believe it was when he was praying to God in Gethsemane while sweating blood that his lofty solitude reached its peak.

He already knew he was destined to die on the cross. But his disciples were fast asleep, not knowing anything. He prayed three times: "Take this cup away from me. Nevertheless, not what I will, but what you will." At that time, God did not answer Jesus.

This is what I think: Jesus was aware that he was a savior and the son of God. But even Jesus agonized over his wish to live as a human and had a glimpse of doubt as to why God wouldn't save him by making a miracle at the last moment as He did with prophets in the past.

He was aware he was a savior, but he also knew his fate of being put to death along with criminals the next day. Was there anyone, even one person, who had ever experienced such a contradiction of life? Precisely at that moment, Jesus was at the peak of lofty solitude—or total isolation—and was standing alone on untrodden ground. When I think of the time when one is forsaken by the world, I cannot forget the image of Jesus praying and sweating blood in Gethsemane.

Looking back on the history of humankind, there are probably more people than one can count on fingers who experienced the lofty isolation of standing alone on untrodden ground. Galileo, who was put on trial for advocating the theory of heliocentrism, was one such example. Magellan, who planned to circumnavigate the globe by ship, also must have felt solitude when he saw no one sided with him. Lincoln, too, must have felt the same at the great moment when he finally decided to emancipate the slaves—the loneliness particular to only those who have witnessed the moments that determined the destiny of humankind.

Another case is Shoin Yoshida[2], who died at the young age of 28. He rowed a small boat on a pitch-black night from Shimoda, Japan, to board a black American ship off the coast, as he was determined to go to the United States. When he started rowing the boat, determined to create a brighter future for Japan, I imagine he must have felt the lofty solitude of standing alone on untrodden ground.

The time when you are forsaken by the world is a time of sadness. It is at this time of sadness, however, that your soul is being tested. It is also a moment that will inspire the later generations. When you are forsaken by the world, you stand empty-handed. There is nothing to adorn you, and there is no one to side with you. However, platinum shines most brilliantly when it is put in blazing fire. When you feel you are forsaken by the world, perhaps you should ask yourself if you are standing at a turning point in life or are in a revolutionary period for humanity.

[Memo]
the third case   untrodden ground
no teacher in life   all alone

To My Wife-to-Be

May 27, 1984

Dear wife-to-be, I still don't know who you are. You may be someone I've already met, and perhaps you are looking at me with your lovely, sparkling eyes, thinking, "Oh, he's so slow. Why can't he realize I'm the one to be his wife?" Or maybe I've yet to meet you, and you are taking a stroll along the beach in the May breeze.

Dear wife-to-be, whoever you are, I send my love to the future you. I hope that some years from now, you will unexpectedly find this short essay as you tidy up my desk and cannot help but feel love for me with nostalgia—me on a day when I was 27 years old.

Dear wife-to-be, I believe in spiritual bonds, although this may not go with today's sense of things. I simply believe there is a woman who is promised to be my wife even before my birth. I simply believe that invisible threads of God's Will stretch throughout this world and that those who are linked by fate will steadily be brought together. Won't you agree? Some may say that out of tens or hundreds of millions of men and women who are born into this world in the same generation, a pair of a man and a woman is formed just by sheer luck. But wouldn't it be better to think that we had known each other long before this country Japan even came into existence and that we had promised each other to be born in the same 20th-century Japan and to live a life of love and service to many people by helping each other as husband and wife? Wouldn't this make our meeting more wonderful?

Dear wife-to-be, I, who am to be your husband, am firmly determined to live a life of love and service to others. Hopefully, you too will resolve to be a light of this world and to light up one corner of the world, even a little.

Dear wife-to-be, the life of a human being is like a short-lived sparkler, of only 60–70 years. But let us make good use of this little opportunity that

God has given us to make our souls shine brighter. Let us use this limited time to make people happy.

Dear wife-to-be, I once read this story. A man had a dream. In it, well-known philosophers and saints were gathering in the world of God, each admiring the brightly shining diamond called Truth. However, one of the philosophers carelessly let the diamond of Truth slip from his hand. It fell onto the earth and shattered into small pieces. People on the earth picked up the small fragments of the diamond, each claiming that the piece they found is the world's best diamond of Truth.

Dear wife-to-be, do you understand the meaning of this dream? Each small piece of the fallen and scattered diamond is called Christianity in one place, Buddhism in another place, Greek philosophy in yet another, and Confucianism and modern German idealistic philosophy elsewhere.

Dear wife-to-be, my work in this world is to pick up all the scattered pieces of the diamond and let people know and believe that the real diamond of Truth is far bigger and far more wonderful than these small pieces. Picking up all the pieces is a challenging task, and I would like a little help from you, too. I'm sure you will be willing.

Dear wife-to-be, I look forward to that day, that beautiful moment, when you will appear before me.

As Moomin

May 27, 1984

It has been two months since I moved to Nagoya. The housemother of the company dormitory has a daughter, and she gave me the nickname "Moomin." It is a name taken after the title character of the animated TV show *The Moomins*. I don't know if Moomin is a hippo or a legendary dream-eating creature, *baku*, since I don't know much about it. Nonetheless, hippos live in rivers and swamps, but the Moomins live in the Moominvalley, so I think they are perhaps *baku* and not hippos.

It was probably because of my appearance or voice that the daughter started saying I resembled Moomin. But thinking twice, maybe Moomin's character is also similar to mine. Moomin is always living as if he were dreaming. He is shy, optimistic, and simply believes what others say. Although he is not good-looking, that gives us a strange sense of comfort. After all, I think it is not bad to be called Moomin.

If the world was full of people like Moomin, we could have peaceful and happy days, although we would not make any rapid progress. Moomin does not get angry or hate others. Moomin does not speak ill of others or say bad things behind someone's back. On rainy days, he dreams of sunny weather, and on sunny days, he enjoys being in the sun. Moomin does not complain. He only thinks about having fun in his life.

Like Moomin, I want to live while dreaming. Like Moomin, I want to live while being innocent and loving peace. Like Moomin, I want to live while loving others and being loved by others. (A recent spiritual message revealed that Moomin is an avatar of the God Odin of Northern Europe.)

CHAPTER FIVE

Love and the Spirit World

On the Salvation of Evil Spirits (1)

May 13, 1984

The first puzzling question for people who believe in God and who believe that God created this world is the existence of evil spirits.

Of course, evil spirits cannot be seen by the ordinary human eye. Moreover, because the writings that describe evil spirits are always frightening and creepy, people tend to misunderstand the spiritual world as a mere eerie realm. As a result, it is sometimes said to be superstition, and at other times, it is dismissed as unscientific.

However, for those who have opened their spiritual sight, evil spirits do indeed exist; they clearly perceive that evil spirits are a group of spirits that makes up the bottom part of the Spirit World.

First, I will talk about the characteristics of evil spirits based on my own experience.

The first category of evil spirits is animal spirits. Among the spirits of dead animals, there are those that wander into the human realm and cause different kinds of disturbances. In a way, these spirits are miserable; they do not have the opportunity to encounter the Truth as humans do, and they do not recognize the difference between body and spirit or the boundary between life and death. Even if you were to communicate with them through automatic writing, they will only tell you what spirits they are or complain that they are in pain or are hungry.

The animal spirits I have met so far include the spirits of snakes that were killed, the spirits of dogs, the spirits of pigs, and most commonly, the spirits of foxes.

The characteristic of these spirits is their strong feelings of grudge, hatred, and greed. From what I observed, in many cases, snake spirits possess people with intense feelings of hatred and anger. I have only seen two cases of people possessed by dog spirits. One of them was living a very sloppy life that reminded others of the life of a stray dog. The other was possessed by not a simple dog spirit but a vicious one that could be regarded as an "Inugami" (literally, "dog deity") worshipped in some regions of Japan. This man had a tendency of stealing; he would always be nervously looking around and was disliked and shunned by others.

"Clinically," fox spirits were the spirits I most commonly dealt with. I think this is because a kind of spiritual magnetic field has been formed in Japan due to the Japanese tradition of *Inari* (fox deity) worship. The distinct feature of fox spirits is that they often possess people who are in unfortunate circumstances and are religious at the same time. Without realizing they are possessed, these people visit shrines that worship *Inari* and tend to adore eating fresh fish, shrimps, crabs, squillas, and the like.

I think if this world is God's creation, it is unreasonable to think that only human beings have both a spirit and a body and that the other animals only have a body. I think it's more logical to assume that all living creatures in this third dimensional world are imbued with God's breath;

in this sense, they are "living" and have souls. The awareness of animal spirits is of course low; there is a considerable gap in awareness between human spirits and animal spirits. But they, too, are at least given a chance to achieve the minimum level of enlightenment, which is to know the difference between life and death and to understand that happiness means living in harmony with others.

The second category of evil spirits is the human spirits that do not know they are dead. Oftentimes, people who have died from sudden deaths come to have an unusually strong attachment to this world of phenomena. When people who do not believe in the afterlife die from an accident or illness, they have no choice but to rely on their family members and relatives and come to live with them. But their interference has various negative influences, causing physical disorders or amplifying various bad feelings in the living people; they end up making the living unhappy. In many cases, these spirits have no intention of making their dearest people unhappy, but because they are so desperate to be saved, they end up disturbing the spiritual training that living people are carrying out in their physical bodies. The only way for the living people to save these evil spirits is to live cheerfully and happily with correct religious beliefs and inspire them with such a way of life.

The third category of evil spirits is the so-called spirits of hell. When they had a human life on earth, they lived in a way that went against their mission as children of God, so they are unable to return to heaven. These spirits of hell are classified in various ways—for example, as in Dante's *Divine Comedy* in the West or generally in the philosophy of hell in the East. I do not have enough time and space to explain it all, but the following are some of the typical spirits in hell.

(1) The Spirits of the Asura Hell

These spirits have the mental traits of being belligerent, destructive, and distrustful of other human beings.

They often secretly control and manipulate the people who are excessively competitive, who bad-mouth others, and who hurt others.

(2) The Spirits of the Hell of Lust

In today's world, sexual freedom has increased. There are various movements to promote sexual liberation, such as advancements in birth control methods, the promotion of gender equality, the collapse of the family system, and the practice of artificial insemination. We cannot say all of these are wrong. However, sexual activity tends to make people more conscious of their flesh rather than awaken them as spirits. In this sense, indulging in carnal desire goes against human nature as children of God, and it makes people more susceptible to the influence of the evil spirits of the same nature. The fact that the spirits of the Hell of Lust exist shows that carnal desire does not accord with God's Laws.

(3) The Spirits of the Hell of Villains

These are the spirits of the so-called gangsters, rogues, and the like, or of people who have lost their noble character as children of God and have violent vibrations. As in the saying, "Like attracts like," they possess violent people. It is the awareness as a child of God and the awareness of their holy mission that will save them.

(4) The Spirits of the Hell of Beasts

The Hell of Beasts is the destination of those who lived like animals, who lacked the awareness of human beings, children of God. They do not know love, do not know God, do not understand what it is to be human, and are only living on instincts. Sometimes they can appear in a form that could make those with spiritual sight mistakenly see them as real animal spirits. They are the evil spirits of those who have fallen to the so-called Hell of Beasts.

(5) The Spirits of the Abysmal Hell

The Abysmal Hell is where misguiding religious leaders, scholars, thinkers, politicians, and others who have led many people astray go after death. If they fall into a deeper hell, they will join the group of the so-called devils.

There are also other spirits in hell, but because they can be found in other references, I will not go into their details here.

The fourth category of evil spirits includes what is generally called devils and satans. Of course, even satans were previously humans; when they lived on earth as human beings, they defied their mission as children of God and then fell to hell. As they lived in hell for a long time, they gained power as inhabitants of hell and are now actively trying to delude even the people on earth. Some of them were originally angels or Buddhist practitioners. They not only have gone astray themselves but also are ruling over other evil spirits using their spiritual power.

We are now living in the Final Days of the Laws, and the vibrations of heaven and hell are clashing on earth. When the right Truth is taught, the guiding spirits who embody God's Will are obstructed in many ways from teaching the Truth. It was the opposition forces by satans that tried to obstruct Shakyamuni Buddha's enlightenment, manipulated people to persecute Jesus, and repeatedly assaulted Nichiren[3].

And now, in this current age, devils are trying to hinder my enlightenment by inflicting on me various kinds of physical and mental pain and are trying to obstruct my spiritual channeling. Among them are Beelzebub, who appeared in September 1981, Lucifer, who appeared in October of the same year, and Kakuban, who used to be a monk of esoteric Buddhism. Kakuban first appeared in May 1982 and has been trying me for nearly two years now (as of May 1984).

Unlike the other spirits in hell, these satans have a clear intention of proactively obstructing the Kingdom of God from being built. However, even they are to be saved at some point in eternal time. They fell to hell because of the earthly world, not because of the heavenly world, so we can only save them through this earthly world. To be more specific, the only ways to save them are to cut off the source of energy that is feeding hell by creating the Kingdom of God on earth, to guide them to reflect on their deeds and thoughts and to inspire them. From now on, we must teach the great Laws that will purify even the satans in hell.

On the Salvation of Evil Spirits (2)

Morning of May 14, 1984

Hell is not just an idea but a reality. And evil spirits are actually leading living people astray. These realities give rise to the questions: Did God create hell? Did He also create the spirits of hell? Why doesn't He eliminate hell?

The answer I have reached so far is that hell was created not by God but by human beings who have been using Earth as a place of spiritual training through repeated reincarnations over a long time. Hell was created based on the law of retributive justice—the famous law that states, "As you sow, so shall you reap." To explain this further, people who lived with hatred during their lives on earth, for example, are destined to eventually realize that their hatred was wrong by meeting others in hell with similar hatred.

The law "you must reap what you sow" applies to the individual and also to humanity as a whole.

Because human beings have created hell through their lives on earth, it must be eliminated through their lives on earth. That is why God does not try to destroy hell all at once. He is expecting humanity to make efforts to purify the earth and eventually turn the realm of hell into the realm of light.

Hell is like a hospital in the Spirit World. The patients there are sick souls. Some people may ask why God just leaves evil spirits as they are or why God does not just burn them in the hellfire. But I want to ask these people: Are you saying that the sick are no longer human? If human beings mean healthy people, then a sick person may not be called a human being. In reality, however, this is not the case. Everyone can get sick. Even if a person gets sick because of their carelessness or some external cause, we try to save the sick, don't we?

Evil spirits are souls that are suffering from illness. The reason why God is patiently waiting for them to get back on their feet is the same as why we pray for the recovery of the sick. The reason why God allows them to exist is the same as why we approve for the sick to live.

It is not God who created the sick. God created healthy human beings. Although a healthy person can get sick, they will eventually be cured of illness. In the same way, let us think of hell as a hospital. Let us think of evil spirits as sick souls. They can be revived as healthy souls with the medicine called "enlightenment." No matter how selfish and full of themselves these evil spirits may be, just as sick people often are, let us admonish them, encourage them, guide them in the right direction, and save them, like doctors or the families of the sick. For that is also how our souls can make progress.

On the Salvation of Evil Spirits (3)

Evening of May 14, 1984

I said that evil spirits are souls suffering from illness. So what part of their soul is ailing? How can we treat the sick without knowing what is wrong?

The first characteristic they have in common is the lack of love. They do not know how wonderful love is. They do not know the real meaning of truly thinking about others in their shoes, truly acting for others, being truly kind to others, or truly serving others. They do not know the joy of guiding others in the right direction or the real excitement and selfless pleasure of life they can feel when they are working to help others grow. They do not know that love is the purpose of life, that love is what helps them to improve, that love is the only power, and that love is the boat of salvation that takes them out of hell and into heaven. Evil spirits do not know that just as there is gravitation on Earth, human beings, who are the children of God, are governed by the "gravitation of love" that attracts all to each other. Evil spirits suffer because they try to live while going against this gravitation of love. Because they try to defy this law of the universe, as a reaction, they meet with consequences that make them suffer. In this sense, the lack of love also means ignorance of the law.

The second common characteristic of evil spirits is that they are ignorant of the law of reincarnation. Human beings are living an eternal life given by God. Most evil spirits are obsessed with the feelings that make them say, "I wanted to enjoy physical life more" or "I didn't want to die." However, they do not know the Truth. Human beings can never die. Even if they wanted to, they can never die forever.

Just as planet Earth continues to revolve around the Sun, human life goes back and forth forever between the Real World and this phenomenal world while constantly changing its phases. Human beings are life forms that are born on earth in the cycle of every tens of years, hundreds of years, or thousands of years, depending on the person.

How can evil spirits understand this magnificent Truth of the universe? If we are fellow humans who came here on earth after tens of thousands, hundreds of thousands, or even hundreds of millions of years of repeated reincarnations, why should we hate, hurt, or kill each other? No matter how painful one's earthly life might be, the suffering of just 60 or 70 years goes by in a blink of an eye from the perspective of eternal life. No matter what hardships may come our way, they are just the whetstones to polish our lives and make them shine.

The third common characteristic of evil spirits is that they do not have the correct outlook on the world. They do not understand the difference between this third dimensional, phenomenal world and the multidimensional Real World extending from the fourth dimension and beyond. That is why they get lost after they die.

In this third dimensional world, we undergo spiritual training in our physical bodies. And the multidimensional world that extends from the fourth dimension onward is the world of spirits. Spirits can visit this third dimensional world because they are inhabitants of the world of the fourth dimension and beyond. But the theory of physics states that we cannot visit the world beyond this third dimension.

Evil spirits must know that this third dimension is a world of its own and that they must undergo further spiritual training in the Spirit World, which extends from the fourth dimension onward. They are lost in many ways because they have no idea where they belong.

The fourth common characteristic of evil spirits is that they do not know they are children of God. The proof that human beings are children of God is that all people have the ability to love and to be loved; that all people have a conscience and cannot lie to themselves, although they may lie to others; and that all people innately know the true nature of what is good. The awareness of being a child of God will present an evil spirit with a moment to return to its true self.

On Spiritual Stages and on Equality

May 20, 1984

Based on what I hear from the inhabitants of the Spirit World, their worlds are clearly divided into different stages based on their levels of awareness. Why is there such a distinct hierarchy in the Real World created by God? If the Spirit World is God's creation, wouldn't it be enough for all souls to live harmoniously in love and peace in just one place? Why are there realms of different stages in the Real World? I think this is one of the serious issues.

Conventional religions have seen the earthly world we live in as a temporary world and the afterworld as the Real World (the other world). However, as I kept on analyzing the messages from the Spirit World, I began to feel that it is somewhat unreasonable to recognize the entire afterworld as the Real World. That is because even in the world called the Real World, there are realms of real sufferings below the earthly world as well as noble realms where inhabitants are less and less conscious of earthly life. So first I would like to describe the different stages in the afterworld, as far as I understand.

(1) The Fourth Dimensional World (the Astral Realm and Hell)

The fourth dimensional world is close to our third dimensional world, so its inhabitants have very strong earthly feelings. Usually, the spirits have shed their physical bodies and live in this fourth dimensional world as astral bodies. These spirits are characterized by the fact that they have not sufficiently realized they are dead. Or even if they are slightly aware that they have died, they are not aware that they are children of God and that the world was created by God.

Among the souls of the dead, those who are not much tainted by evil and who wish to continue to live their earthly lives form the world called the

Astral Realm and inhabit it. On the other hand, those who are tainted by evil, who need to cleanse away their evil, who continue to grieve or complain of pain even after death, and who continue to strongly cling to their earthly lives make up the realm of hell.

There are different stages in hell as well. In a relatively shallow place is the Hell of Villains and others, whereas the Abysmal Hell is located in the deepest place. Such different stages exist. The Hell of Villains is inhabited by those who posed a threat to other people's ordinary lives or endangered others' physical lives, such as gangsters. In contrast, the Abysmal Hell is inhabited by those who corrupted other people's souls, which are the very lives of the children of God, through false ideas, beliefs, and religions, or those who distorted God's Laws. They are suffering there out of their own sense of sin.

(2) The Fifth Dimensional World
   (the Spirit World in a narrow sense,
   or the Goodness Realm)

In a broad sense, both heaven and hell are the Spirit World, but I would call the fifth dimensional world the Spirit World in a narrow sense. Most of the inhabitants of the fifth dimension had first entered the Astral Realm after death and were brought up to this Spirit World after having been more or less aware that human beings are children of God. Those who lived as good citizens on earth live in communities in this Spirit World. However, they still do not fully know God's Truth and are learning the Truth from those of the higher realms.

(3) The Sixth Dimensional World
   (the Light Realm)

This realm and the realms above it are often referred to as the heavenly world. The inhabitants have their own areas of expertise, and they are a group of specialists who are working to bring light to the earthly world. Among them are scholars, artists, and religious leaders who still stop at the level of moralists.

One of the inhabitants of this Light Realm is Murasaki Shikibu[4], a pioneering Japanese novelist. According to her spiritual messages, she now lives alone in a house situated in a scenic location similar to a Japanese suburb. She says she lives a simple life—watering the flowers in her garden, attending weekly meetings of her fellow writers' group, and shopping in a sort of supermarket while dressed in modern clothes. When shopping, she does not use money but offers a feeling of gratitude equivalent to the items she purchases. She says that the one who receives her gratitude gets rich by the amount of gratitude they get. There are also cars and TV sets, and the TV broadcasts include the news of the Spirit World.

I once asked her if the love between a man and a woman also exists in the Light Realm because she had written a novel on this theme, and her reply was as follows: Sometimes when they meet a nice member of the opposite sex on the street or in a meeting, they may feel admiration or feel excited, which might be called a romantic feeling, but there is not much sexual sense in it. They always think about the love for God and the love from God, and the love of human beings feels less attractive to them.

We can say that this sixth dimensional world is composed of the spirits who are more or less aware of them being leaders in their own fields. But even this Light Realm is divided into the upper, middle, and lower stages according to strict standards. The upper stage of the Light Realm is inhabited by the light of angels called various deities. They continue their spiritual training to advance into yet higher realms while also teaching God's Laws in plain language to the inhabitants of the Light Realm and below. The enlightenment of those in the Light Realm is, in a nutshell, the enlightenment of intellect or the enlightenment in the field of philosophy or ethical philosophy.

In addition, this Light Realm has a rear side called Rear Heaven. It is part of the sixth dimension but is inhabited by those who have attained enlightenment through austere ascetic training while they were alive in the phenomenal world. They became enlightened through physical practice and not through intellectual pursuits as others do. The Rear Heaven has the Tengu (long-nosed goblins) Realm and the Sennin (hermit sorcerers) Realm. In other words, it is the world of psychics. Many of its inhabitants were religious practitioners while they lived on earth, but they misunderstood their psychic powers for enlightenment and are unable to reach the world of true love and compassion of God or Buddha. These spirits often guide the people who practice hypnosis, astrology, onomancy, magic, or psychic healing on earth.

(4) The Seventh Dimensional World
(the Bodhisattva Realm)

Whereas the sixth dimension is made up of those who have attained the enlightenment of intellect or of physical practice, the seventh dimension comprises those who have attained the enlightenment of love. Love surpasses knowledge and power. In other words, the enlightenment of the seventh dimension can be expressed as the enlightenment of Mahayana (greater vehicle), which transcends the sixth dimensional enlightenment of Hinayana (lesser vehicle). We can at least say that the inhabitants of this Bodhisattva Realm all think of living for the sake of others.

When a tathagata[5] teaches the Laws on earth, the inhabitants of the Bodhisattva Realm are born on earth to help convey the Laws to many people. Bodhisattvas are also born on earth in groups to revive God's Laws. Other than religious leaders, they are also born as scholars, artists, or politicians to bring about advancement to the age.

Some of the well-known bodhisattvas born in Japan are religious leaders such as Nichiren, Shinran[6], and Kukai. Ryoma Sakamoto[7], Chomin Nakae[8], Kanzo Uchimura[9], and Tadao Yanaihara[10], who were born more recently, are also bodhisattvas. (To be continued.)

[Memo]
Equality at the basis of existence and equality for evolutionary purposes

On Spiritual Freedom

May 16, 1984 (1)
May 20, 1984 (2)

(1) Freedom to Create

God has given human beings freedom—the freedom to create and the freedom to control oneself.

First, as for the freedom to create, God has given human beings the freedom to create a paradise on earth. We humans were already in the Real World before being born on earth. When God sent human beings down to this world, He said, "Humans, live in the flesh on earth. Undergo spiritual training in the flesh. The spiritual training will be tough, but in return, I will grant you a great treasure. That is, I shall give you the freedom of creation to build a paradise on earth. Just as I, God, have created this Real World, you humans shall create a paradise in this third dimensional phenomenal world." Human beings are called children of God because they have been given the freedom of creation, which is one of God's attributes.

Here, I would like you to read God's words carefully. God has granted human beings the freedom to build a paradise. God has entrusted humans with the mission of building a world of great harmony, not a world of struggle and disharmony. God wishes for humans to create a world full of delight and joy.

Contrary to these wishes of God, human beings have repeatedly created a world of tragedy, conflicts, and ugliness throughout their long history. Because these deeds went against their divine nature, human beings have come to be burdened with what is called karma or sin. I repeat: God has given human beings the freedom to create a paradise, the freedom to build a paradise, and in return, human beings have pledged to God to fulfill their duty of creating a paradise on earth.

(2) Freedom to Control Oneself

The second freedom that God has given human beings is the freedom to control themselves. Atheists often skeptically ask, "If God is perfect and flawless, why does evil prevail in this world? Why is there no end to the number of evildoers?" In response to these questions, I would answer that God has given humans the freedom to control themselves.

One of the light of guiding spirits explained this to me as follows: If human beings are likened to salmon that return to the rivers of their birth and swim upstream to spawn, then it is God's supreme command to them to swim upstream to spawn. To swim upstream means to return to the bosom of God and to move toward what is good. That is why God has given salmon (human beings in their physical bodies) the habit of swimming upstream. However, being given this habit does not mean salmon cannot swim downstream by their own free will.

Some people may question: "God could have created human beings to do only good and never do evil, but why didn't He do so?" But if salmon can only swim upstream, then they would be no different from machines; they would merely be God's robots with no freedom.

Although salmon are supposed to swim upstream, on their journey upstream to spawn, they may float downstream at times or veer off to another stream at other times. In the case of human beings, "swimming downstream" or "veering off course" would mean committing sins. Atoning for the sins means that the salmon must make extra efforts to reach their destination upstream by swimming as much distance as they went downstream or sideways.

In fact, this is explained by the principle of "you must reap what you have sown" or the law of retributive justice. In other words, those who went against God's supreme command to swim upstream must make an extra effort to swim back equivalent to how much they have disobeyed the command.

This is the second freedom that God has given human beings—the freedom to control themselves.

CHAPTER SIX

Love and the Philosophy of Happiness

Abstracts on the Philosophy of Happiness Regarding Recognition and Expression

January 21, 1984

Happiness does not arise from external factors. Happiness is not about material things. Happiness is about our minds. This is true, indeed. Many thinkers and religious leaders have said that happiness is found within ourselves.

I, too, believe that happiness can be found within our minds. To put it another way, the first step to happiness is to recognize that happiness comes depending on our mental attitude and that it will disappear as soon as our mental attitude is distorted. The second step to happiness is to recognize that if our mental attitude changes, then external matters that surround us—even the material environment—will also change. Truly, people with a wealthy heart will be blessed with a wealthy environment.

However, both the first recognition—happiness depends on one's mental attitude—and the second recognition—a happy situation will also arise externally depending on one's mental attitude—are not assured at this point. This is because recognition is changeable and fleeting as long as it remains only as recognition.

To engrave our recognitions onto the memory boards of our minds, we definitely need to express these recognitions. People who can say "I'm happy" out loud are already happy. Those who can show a big smile of happiness on their faces are already happy. Strangely enough, even though we need to express ourselves to confirm our recognition of being happy, it is through our expressions that we can better recognize our happiness. Here, we come to discover that three elements—recognition, mental attitude, and expression—form a cycle to create a magnetic field called happiness.

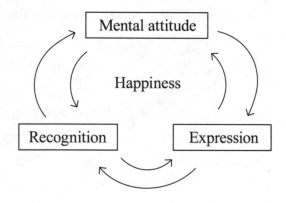

Happiness and Time

Those who wish to live happily must not disregard the first and most basic principle: we exist within time, which flows throughout the magnificent space of heaven and earth. All the elements that produce our happiness and unhappiness are shining in the flow of time, like the innumerable stars in the Milky Way. It is as if various stars are giving colors to make our lives either brighter or darker, sometimes by concentrating and sometimes by dispersing.

So first the people who wish to live happily must realize that all the elements that shape their happiness lie in the flow of the time of their lives and that the key to their happiness is to be found in how the various elements concentrate and disperse through the medium of time. Both joy and sorrow lie in the flow of time. Of all the things we can experience as human beings, nothing can escape from the flow of time. All love, all hatred, all hope, and all despair will be floating and sinking as they are washed down the great flow of time.

Moreover, those who aim to be happy will probably agree that time is alive in a sense; it mainly flows from the present to the past, but sometimes it wanders around a point in the present or even flows backward from the present to the future or from the past to the future. This is the second principle regarding happiness and time. In other words, time is alive, and as long as it is alive, it can move into the past or into the future. Don't you agree?

Think about it. Isn't it true that ripples caused by a pebble thrown into the pond of time that has already passed can affect you who are living in the present as well as you who will live in the future? Isn't it true that the pebble of happiness or unhappiness to be thrown in the future is causing ripples affecting you in the present or in the past?

The living creature called "time" is like an inchworm. It can crawl toward the past or the future, or it can hunch on one spot. Let's say one of us made a mistake in the past. If the person continues to agonize over the mistake believing there is nothing they can do about it, an inchworm called "time" will stick to that point in the past and will not move an inch. At such times, no matter how much time as measured by a clock goes by, the person is not living in the present, nor will they live in the future, but is living at that point of time in the past.

Let me take another example. Suppose an unmarried woman is constantly dreaming of a happy married life. If this thought is occupying her mind all day long, then the inchworm of her time has already started to crawl toward the future, trying to hunch on one point in the future.

Here we can find the third and fourth principles regarding happiness and time.

The third principle is that whereas time, as indicated by the hands of a clock, moves forward equally for each person and is irreversible, time in connection to happiness is not only reversible, as stated by the second principle, but also unique to each person. In other words, time in relation to happiness is unique to each individual because it is entirely up to each person's mental inclination to decide which way the inchworm of time will move. Some people are absorbed in the present, whereas others are only concerned with the pleasures or worries of the future.

The fourth principle is that the primary concern of each individual will affect their time regarding happiness. In other words, whether a person lives in the past, the future, or the present is determined by their primary concern or by what matters most to them. For those who are in deep disappointment, their inchworm of time just sticks to that one point in the past when the painful event took place. In such situations, these people will pay less and less attention to what happens in their daily lives. As they monotonously carry out their work in their office, ironically, their wristwatch will inform them of lunchtime and the bell will eventually ring to tell them it is time for them to go home.

As stated above, we have four principles regarding happiness and time. The first principle is that all the factors affecting happiness are in the flow of time. The second principle is that time concerning happiness is reversible; it can flow from the present to the past and from the past to the future. The third principle is that time concerning happiness is unique to and dependent on each individual. And the fourth principle is that the primary concern of each person determines their time regarding happiness.

Now, we must go further and push open the door to happiness. Because our entire existence *was* in time, *is* in time now, and *will be* in time in the future, don't we need to take complete control over the flow of time and live in such a time where we are always blessed with happiness?

To be happy, what kind of time should you live? Just because you were unhappy in the past does not mean you should be miserable in the present. More so, you should not let past misery cast a shadow over your future. If you live in anxiety in the present just because you fear the future, what is the meaning of the present time? You can instead remember beautiful events of the past and project them into the future. There is no need to lament not having a dream or hope in the present. You can find your major concern in the bright future events and live in that time, or you can live in a golden time of the past.

The past, present, and future are a single point. In our minds, they are just one point. Time becomes a single point when contracted and infinite when expanded. This is the true nature of time. Even unhappiness that seems to linger from the past into the future can be contracted into a single point in the great flow of time. Yes, compress your misfortune into a single point in the past and let the inchworm of the time eat it. You can push your fear of the future away to a single point and let your inchworm of time dance happily in the present.

On the other hand, the events that bring you happiness are also a single point in the flow of time. But you can expand that point so that it runs through the past, present, and future. If you make the wonderful events of the past your primary concern and let the inchworm of time hunch on that spot, a bright ray of light shall illuminate the path for you now and in the future.

The past, present, and future are a single point. They are a single point when contracted and infinite when expanded. Adjust the flow of time yourself by confining unhappiness to a single point while expanding happiness to infinity; there you will find the path to happiness.

Existence and Love

August 4, 1984

Have you ever pondered over "existence"? What we can see with our eyes and recognize the shape, or what we can feel with our hands—are they truly real? If what we can see with our eyes and touch with our hands is real, then what about the things we see and touch in our dreams? Can we recognize the things in our dreams as existence?

In our dreams, we often perceive something as existence without being aware we are dreaming. But how do we know whether the things we recognize as existence through our five senses, including seeing, hearing, and touching, are real existences? How do we know that the time we commonly share when we are awake is not time in a dream from the perspective of a higher dimension?

I think what makes existence "existence" is an idea. Everything we perceive as existing is the manifestation of an idea. For example, we call a certain kind of creature a "dog" and a particular thing a "stone," even though there is no guarantee that each person sees exactly the same thing. We just call it a dog or a stone; it's not because of how long, wide, or tall it is, how it moves, or what kind of sound it makes. A dog is still a dog, even if it is missing an ear or a leg. From this, we can see that it is not necessarily our perception that makes what we perceive an "existence."

If we define "existence" as the manifestation of a particular idea, can we also recognize spiritual matters—not material things—as "existences"? We can certainly say that spiritual matters also embody particular ideas. The question is whether spiritual matters have the form to be objectively recognized as "existences." If spiritual matters are given the form to be recognized as objectively as we recognize stones as "existences" by hearing the word "stone," then I believe spiritual matters can also be recognized as "existences."

So can we say that love—the most important spiritual element of human beings—is an "existence"?

Love indeed embodies a specific idea. For some, it is the working of God Himself; for others, it is the central concept of God's ethical order: "Love one another." When the word "love" was born, it surely became an "existence" as an idea.

Then, does love have a form to be objectively recognized to the same degree as the words "dog" and "stone"? As strong support for an affirmative answer, we can say that the word for "love" exists in various languages regardless of the differences in time, place, and people. This means there is a particular form for love to be recognized as love. Then, which aspect of love makes it possible for love to be perceived as a particular form? This is also a matter of proving love in an objective way.

Does love have objectivity? Is there any objective form of love that can be perceived by all people? Love certainly seems to be subjective in that it is born in every person's heart. That is because we see love as the product of each person's thoughts. But if love is understood as something that has been given *a priori*, or innately, and not as a result of an individual's thoughts, then love is not subjective but definitely objective and can be commonly sensed by all people. In other words, if love is *a priori*, and if we perceive it to be "love" as it manifests at a specific time and place or to a specific person, then we can say love has a form to be recognized objectively.

Then, is love *a priori*? Or did we learn about love for the first time when our parents taught us in our childhood that love means being kind to others? Did people learn about love *a posteriori* when they became Christian and learned Jesus' words: "God is love" or "Love your neighbor as you love yourself"?

My answer is no. Although it is possible to inductively feel love by referring to individual acts of love, we rather recognize what we can deductively know by encountering one or two acts of love in the process of growing up as a human being. Don't you think so? Do we get warm feelings because we were taught that loving others makes us feel that way? I don't think so. It is when we get the warm feelings that we feel for the first time, "Ah, this is love." We innately know what love is, without being taught. When we love someone, we feel the urge to be close to that person; but is this because we have been taught that this happens when we love someone? I don't believe so. When we love someone, a gravitation-like magnetic field is always produced. Isn't this form, this universal, timeless form that always occurs, what we call love?

From the points above, I have come to a conclusion: love is an existence because it is the manifestation of a particular idea and because it has a form to be objectively recognized. Love is an existence. Not only that, love is an existence that is universally recognized, transcending time and place.

Epilogue

Because We Are Human

July 8, 1984

Feelings of helplessness, impatience, inferiority, self-deprecation, lack of self-confidence, indecisiveness, unpleasant feelings, anxiety, fear of the unknown, lamentation, sadness, and pain—such seeds of unhappiness that came out of Pandora's box make human beings worry and become weak.

However, no matter how much we look at the seeds of unhappiness, we will only see unhappiness grow and can hardly be happy. To be happy, we must look for the seeds of happiness.

Because we are human, there are countless things we can do.

I can breathe.

I can yawn big and wide.

I can see the view from the window.

I can walk.

I can run, too.

I can sleep.

I can smell a flower.

I can listen to the sound of a stream.

I can play catch.

I can lie on the grass.

I can make a mound in the sand.

I can climb a hill and watch the morning sun.

I can get up early.

I can believe in Santa Claus.

I can talk with my father and my mother.

I can learn various things.

I can say hello.

I can make a smile.

I can shake hands.

I can think.

I can look up at the Milky Way.

I can have a meal.

I can snap my fingers.

I can fall on my bottom.

I can run down a hill.

I can play with the breeze.

I can make friends with dogs.

I can be a friend.

I can feel happy.

I can drink cold juice.

I can fall in love.

I can wear nice clothes.

I can love people.

I can be loved by people.

I can believe in God.

I can...

Because we are human, we are promised many wonderful things. Because we are human, we can do so many things. Because we are human, we have so much freedom. Because we are human, we can live a brilliant life. Because we are human...

Figures

Present

What Are the Unchanging (Universal) Things?

1. Human beings are animals that live in constant pursuit of happiness.

2. Economic activity to sustain livelihood will remain as a bare necessity.

3. Love between men and women.
   (Love between parents and children, love between brothers and sisters, love between teachers and students, and love between compatriots will probably change.)

4. The seeking of rest.

5. Having various forms of stimulation to prevent boredom (the need of entertainment).

Future

6. There will be men and women,
   the young and the old.

7. The differences in the degree of spiritual life.

8. The different sizes of bodies, and the different
   degrees of physical strength.

9. Measures to differentiate human beings.

The Universal Things (Continued)

10. Human beings are not exempt from worries, sufferings, or anxieties.

11. Human beings cannot live alone, and must coexist with others.

12. Human beings usually live less than 100 years, and there are only 24 hours in a day.

13. Human beings crave a sense of importance and love.

14. Human beings must be conscious of the eyes of others as they live.

15. Human beings give influence on others
    in some way as they live.

16. Each person always has their own unique
    views on life and the world.

17. Human beings live in relativity such as
    good and evil, beauty and ugliness, etc.

18. There are always those who lead
    and those who are led (cf. 7).

The Construction of Love

○ <u>The construction of love</u>

○ <u>What love is for</u>

[Society of Love Incarnate] ⟨ Utopia
Truth
Oneness with
the universe ⟩

↑

[Society of Forgiving Love] ⟨ Tolerance ⟩

↑

[Society of Nurturing Love] ⟨ Growth
Progress ⟩

↑

[Society of Fundamental Love] ⟨ Empathy ⟩

Happiness in Recognition and
Happiness in Real Existence

○ Love is the basis of happiness, and
happiness further produces love.

○ Happiness in relative time and happiness
in absolute time

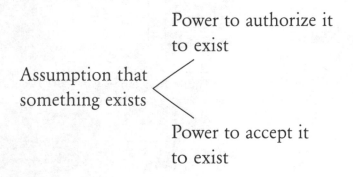

Assumption that something exists

- Power to authorize it to exist
- Power to accept it to exist

On Ideal Society

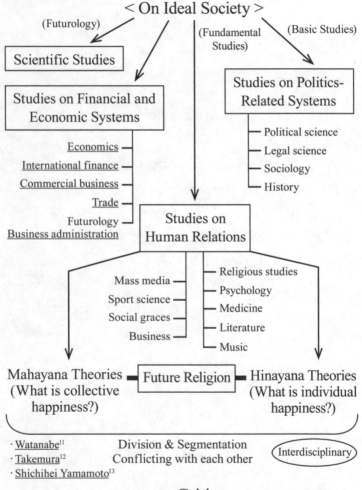

< On Ideal Society >

(Futurology)

Scientific Studies

(Fundamental Studies)

(Basic Studies)

Studies on Financial and Economic Systems

Economics
International finance
Commercial business
Trade
Futurology
Business administration

Studies on Politics-Related Systems

— Political science
— Legal science
— Sociology
— History

Studies on Human Relations

Mass media
Sport science
Social graces
Business

— Religious studies
— Psychology
— Medicine
— Literature
— Music

Mahayana Theories
(What is collective happiness?)

Future Religion

Hinayana Theories
(What is individual happiness?)

· Watanabe[11]
· Takemura[12]
· Shichihei Yamamoto[13]

Division & Segmentation
Conflicting with each other

Interdisciplinary

<u>**Critics**</u> cover these fields.

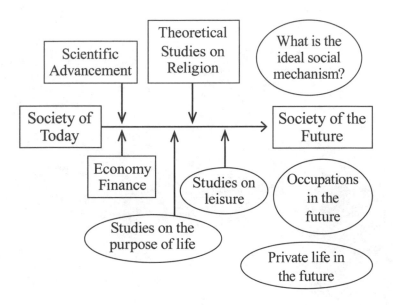

Afterword

I think it is important to show the starting point of my thoughts. Although Happy Science is thought to have begun with a collection of spiritual messages from various spiritual beings, I myself clearly had a starting point—the philosophy of love I expounded during my youth.

I am so happy to be able to reveal these essays on "love and the philosophy of happiness."

There is a profound meaning in how this book begins with my short essay written in New York.

A businessman working for an international trading house was contemplating the "monism of love"—how can such a person be described?

My physical body was in the third dimensional world, but my mind was trying to soar up infinitely high.

With this, the significance of the anniversary year will be completed.

Ryuho Okawa
Master & CEO of Happy Science Group
September 19, 2021

TRANSLATOR'S NOTES

1 Kukai [774 – 835]
Japanese Buddhist monk and the founder of Shingon school of Buddhism.

2 Shoin Yoshida [1830 – 1859]
Japanese samurai who led to bring about the Meiji Restoration by providing a spiritual backbone.

3 Nichiren [1222 – 1282]
Japanese Buddhist monk and the founder of Nichiren school of Buddhism. He warned of the imminent national crisis and criticized other religious groups, which invited persecution from the government and other religious groups.

4 Murasaki Shikibu
One of the most prominent writers in the history of Japanese literature. She lived around the latter half of the 10th century to the beginning of the 11th century. She is known for her full-length novel, *The Tale of Genji*, which tells the story of romantic love in courtly life.

5 tathagata
High spirits in the eighth dimension of the Spirit World. Refer to *The Laws of the Sun*.

6 Shinran [1173 – 1263]
Japanese Buddhist monk and the founder of the True Pure Land Buddhism.

7 Ryoma Sakamoto [1836 – 1867]
Japanese samurai and a leading figure who contributed to bringing about the Meiji Restoration.

8 Chomin Nakae [1847 – 1901]
Japanese thinker and politician who became the theoretical leader of the Freedom and People's Rights Movement in Japan.

9 Kanzo Uchimura [1861 – 1930]
Japanese literary man, Christian thinker, and Bible scholar.

10 Tadao Yanaihara [1893 – 1961]
Japanese educator, economist, and Christian leader. He also served as the president of the University of Tokyo.

11 (Shoichi) Watanabe [1930 – 2017]
One of the most prominent Japanese critics and also an English scholar and a historian.

12 (Ken'ichi) Takemura [1930 – 2019]
One of the most prominent Japanese critics and a journalist.

13 Shichihei Yamamoto [1921 – 1991]
A famous Japanese critic.

For a deeper understanding of
Developmental Stages of Love - The Original Theory
see other books below by Ryuho Okawa:

The Laws of the Sun [New York: IRH Press, 2018]

Love, Nurture, and Forgive [Tokyo: HS Press, 2015]

The Ten Principles from El Cantare Volume I [New York: IRH Press, 2022]

ABOUT THE AUTHOR

Founder and CEO of Happy Science Group.

Ryuho Okawa was born on July 7th 1956, in Tokushima, Japan. After graduating from the University of Tokyo with a law degree, he joined a Tokyo-based trading house. While working at its New York headquarters, he studied international finance at the Graduate Center of the City University of New York. In 1981, he attained Great Enlightenment and became aware that he is El Cantare with a mission to bring salvation to all humankind.

In 1986, he established Happy Science. It now has members in over 165 countries across the world, with more than 700 branches and temples as well as 10,000 missionary houses around the world.

He has given over 3,400 lectures (of which more than 150 are in English) and published over 3,000 books (of which more than 600 are Spiritual Interview Series), and many are translated into 40 languages. Along with *The Laws of the Sun* and *The Laws Of Messiah*, many of the books have become best sellers or million sellers. To date, Happy Science has produced 25 movies. The original story and original concept were given by the Executive Producer Ryuho Okawa. He has also composed the lyrics and music of over 450 songs.

Moreover, he is the Founder of Happy Science University and Happy Science Academy (Junior and Senior High School), Founder and President of the Happiness Realization Party, Founder and Honorary Headmaster of Happy Science Institute of Government and Management, Founder of IRH Press Co., Ltd., and the Chairperson of NEW STAR PRODUCTION Co., Ltd. and ARI Production Co., Ltd.

WHAT IS EL CANTARE?

El Cantare means "the Light of the Earth," and is the Supreme God of the Earth who has been guiding humankind since the beginning of Genesis. He is whom Jesus called Father and Muhammad called Allah, and is *Ame-no-Mioya-Gami*, Japanese Father God. Different parts of El Cantare's core consciousness have descended to Earth in the past, once as Alpha and another as Elohim. His branch spirits, such as Shakyamuni Buddha and Hermes, have descended to Earth many times and helped to flourish many civilizations. To unite various religions and to integrate various fields of study in order to build a new civilization on Earth, a part of the core consciousness has descended to Earth as Master Ryuho Okawa.

Alpha is a part of the core consciousness of El Cantare who descended to Earth around 330 million years ago. Alpha preached Earth's Truths to harmonize and unify Earth-born humans and space people who came from other planets.

Elohim is a part of the core consciousness of El Cantare who descended to Earth around 150 million years ago. He gave wisdom, mainly on the differences of light and darkness, good and evil.

Ame-no-Mioya-Gami (Japanese Father God) is the Creator God and the Father God who appears in the ancient literature, *Hotsuma Tsutae*. It is believed that He descended on the foothills of Mt. Fuji about 30,000 years ago and built the Fuji dynasty, which is the root of the Japanese civilization. With justice as the central pillar, Ame-no-Mioya-Gami's teachings spread to ancient civilizations of other countries in the world.

Shakyamuni Buddha was born as a prince into the Shakya Clan in India around 2,600 years ago. When he was 29 years old, he renounced the world and sought enlightenment. He later attained Great Enlightenment and founded Buddhism.

Hermes is one of the 12 Olympian gods in Greek mythology, but the spiritual Truth is that he taught the teachings of love and progress around 4,300 years ago that became the origin of the current Western civilization. He is a hero that truly existed.

Ophealis was born in Greece around 6,500 years ago and was the leader who took an expedition to as far as Egypt. He is the God of miracles, prosperity, and arts, and is known as Osiris in the Egyptian mythology.

Rient Arl Croud was born as a king of the ancient Incan Empire around 7,000 years ago and taught about the mysteries of the mind. In the heavenly world, he is responsible for the interactions that take place between various planets.

Thoth was an almighty leader who built the golden age of the Atlantic civilization around 12,000 years ago. In the Egyptian mythology, he is known as god Thoth.

Ra Mu was a leader who built the golden age of the civilization of Mu around 17,000 years ago. As a religious leader and a politician, he ruled by uniting religion and politics.

ABOUT HAPPY SCIENCE

Happy Science is a global movement that empowers individuals to find purpose and spiritual happiness and to share that happiness with their families, societies, and the world. With more than 12 million members around the world, Happy Science aims to increase awareness of spiritual truths and expand our capacity for love, compassion, and joy so that together we can create the kind of world we all wish to live in.

Activities at Happy Science are based on the Principles of Happiness (Love, Wisdom, Self-Reflection, and Progress). These principles embrace worldwide philosophies and beliefs, transcending boundaries of culture and religions.

Love teaches us to give ourselves freely without expecting anything in return; it encompasses giving, nurturing, and forgiving.

Wisdom leads us to the insights of spiritual truths, and opens us to the true meaning of life and the Will of God (the universe, the highest power, Buddha).

Self-Reflection brings a mindful, nonjudgmental lens to our thoughts and actions to help us find our truest selves—the essence of our souls—and deepen our connection to the highest power. It helps us attain a clean and peaceful mind and leads us to the right life path.

Progress emphasizes the positive, dynamic aspects of our spiritual growth—actions we can take to manifest and spread happiness around the world. It's a path that not only expands our soul growth, but also furthers the collective potential of the world we live in.

PROGRAMS AND EVENTS

The doors of Happy Science are open to all. We offer a variety of programs and events, including self-exploration and self-growth programs, spiritual seminars, meditation and contemplation sessions, study groups, and book events.

Our programs are designed to:
* Deepen your understanding of your purpose and meaning in life
* Improve your relationships and increase your capacity to love unconditionally
* Attain peace of mind, decrease anxiety and stress, and feel positive
* Gain deeper insights and a broader perspective on the world
* Learn how to overcome life's challenges
  ... and much more.

For more information, visit <u>happy-science.org</u>.

CONTACT INFORMATION

Happy Science is a worldwide organization with branches and temples around the globe. For a comprehensive list, visit the worldwide directory at *happy-science.org*. The following are some of the many Happy Science locations:

UNITED STATES AND CANADA

New York
79 Franklin St., New York, NY 10013, USA
Phone: 1-212-343-7972
Fax: 1-212-343-7973
Email: ny@happy-science.org
Website: happyscience-usa.org

New Jersey
66 Hudson St., #2R, Hoboken, NJ 07030, USA
Phone: 1-201-313-0127
Email: nj@happy-science.org
Website: happyscience-usa.org

Chicago
2300 Barrington Rd., Suite #400,
Hoffman Estates, IL 60169, USA
Phone: 1-630-937-3077
Email: chicago@happy-science.org
Website: happyscience-usa.org

Florida
5208 8th St., Zephyrhills, FL 33542, USA
Phone: 1-813-715-0000
Fax: 1-813-715-0010
Email: florida@happy-science.org
Website: happyscience-usa.org

Atlanta
1874 Piedmont Ave., NE Suite 360-C
Atlanta, GA 30324, USA
Phone: 1-404-892-7770
Email: atlanta@happy-science.org
Website: happyscience-usa.org

San Francisco
525 Clinton St. Redwood City, CA
94062, USA
Phone & Fax: 1-650-363-2777
Email: sf@happy-science.org
Website: happyscience-usa.org

Los Angeles
1590 E. Del Mar Blvd., Pasadena, CA
91106, USA
Phone: 1-626-395-7775
Fax: 1-626-395-7776
Email: la@happy-science.org
Website: happyscience-usa.org

Orange County
16541 Gothard St. Suite 104
Huntington Beach, CA 92647
Phone: 1-714-659-1501
Email: oc@happy-science.org
Website: happyscience-usa.org

San Diego
7841 Balboa Ave. Suite #202
San Diego, CA 92111, USA
Phone: 1-626-395-7775
Fax: 1-626-395-7776
E-mail: sandiego@happy-science.org
Website: happyscience-usa.org

Hawaii
Phone: 1-808-591-9772
Fax: 1-808-591-9776
Email: hi@happy-science.org
Website: happyscience-usa.org

Kauai
3343 Kanakolu Street, Suite 5
Lihue, HI 96766, USA
Phone: 1-808-822-7007
Fax: 1-808-822-6007
Email: kauai-hi@happy-science.org
Website: happyscience-usa.org

Toronto

845 The Queensway Etobicoke,
ON M8Z 1N6, Canada
Phone: 1-416-901-3747
Email: toronto@happy-science.org
Website: happy-science.ca

Tokyo

1-6-7 Togoshi, Shinagawa,
Tokyo, 142-0041, Japan
Phone: 81-3-6384-5770
Fax: 81-3-6384-5776
Email: tokyo@happy-science.org
Website: happy-science.org

London

3 Margaret St.London,
W1W 8RE United Kingdom
Phone: 44-20-7323-9255
Fax: 44-20-7323-9344
Email: eu@happy-science.org
Website: www.happyscience-uk.org

Sydney

516 Pacific Highway, Lane Cove North,
2066 NSW, Australia
Phone: 61-2-9411-2877
Fax: 61-2-9411-2822
Email: sydney@happy-science.org

Sao Paulo

Rua. Domingos de Morais 1154,
Vila Mariana, Sao Paulo SP
CEP 04010-100, Brazil
Phone: 55-11-5088-3800
Email: sp@happy-science.org
Website: happyscience.com.br

Jundiai

Rua Congo, 447, Jd. Bonfiglioli
Jundiai-CEP, 13207-340, Brazil
Phone: 55-11-4587-5952
Email: jundiai@happy-science.org

Vancouver

#201-2607 East 49th Avenue,
Vancouver, BC, V5S 1J9, Canada
Phone: 1-604-437-7735
Fax: 1-604-437-7764
Email: vancouver@happy-science.org
Website: happy-science.ca

Seoul

74, Sadang-ro 27-gil, Dongjak-gu,
Seoul, Korea
Phone: 82-2-3478-8777
Fax: 82-2-3478-9777
Email: korea@happy-science.org
Website: happyscience-korea.org

Taipei

No. 89, Lane 155, Dunhua N. Road,
Songshan District, Taipei City 105, Taiwan
Phone: 886-2-2719-9377
Fax: 886-2-2719-5570
Email: taiwan@happy-science.org
Website: happyscience-tw.org

Kuala Lumpur

No 22A, Block 2, Jalil Link Jalan Jalil
Jaya 2, Bukit Jalil 57000,
Kuala Lumpur, Malaysia
Phone: 60-3-8998-7877
Fax: 60-3-8998-7977
Email: malaysia@happy-science.org
Website: happyscience.org.my

Kathmandu

Kathmandu Metropolitan City,
Ward No. 15, Ring Road, Kimdol,
Sitapaila Kathmandu, Nepal
Phone: 977-1-427-2931
Email: nepal@happy-science.org

Kampala

Plot 877 Rubaga Road, Kampala
P.O. Box 34130 Kampala, UGANDA
Phone: 256-79-4682-121
Email: uganda@happy-science.org

The Happiness Realization Party (HRP) was founded in May 2009 by Master Ryuho Okawa as part of the Happy Science Group. HRP strives to improve the Japanese society, based on three basic political principles of "freedom, democracy, and faith," and let Japan promote individual and public happiness from Asia to the world as a leader nation.

1) Diplomacy and Security: Protecting Freedom, Democracy, and Faith of Japan and the World from China's Totalitarianism

Japan's current defense system is insufficient against China's expanding hegemony and the threat of North Korea's nuclear missiles. Japan, as the leader of Asia, must strengthen its defense power and promote strategic diplomacy together with the nations which share the values of freedom, democracy, and faith. Further, HRP aims to realize world peace under the leadership of Japan, the nation with the spirit of religious tolerance.

2) Economy: Early economic recovery through utilizing the "wisdom of the private sector"

Economy has been damaged severely by the novel coronavirus originated in China. Many companies have been forced into bankruptcy or out of business. What is needed for economic recovery now is not subsidies and regulations by the government, but policies which can utilize the "wisdom of the private sector."

For more information, visit en.hr-party.jp

HAPPY SCIENCE ACADEMY
JUNIOR AND SENIOR HIGH SCHOOL

Happy Science Academy Junior and Senior High School is a boarding school founded with the goal of educating the future leaders of the world who can have a big vision, persevere, and take on new challenges.

Currently, there are two campuses in Japan; the Nasu Main Campus in Tochigi Prefecture, founded in 2010, and the Kansai Campus in Shiga Prefecture, founded in 2013.

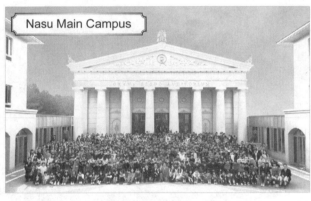

Nasu Main Campus

Kansai Campus

THE FOUNDING SPIRIT AND THE GOAL OF EDUCATION

Based on the founding philosophy of the university, "Exploration of happiness and the creation of a new civilization," education, research and studies will be provided to help students acquire deep understanding grounded in religious belief and advanced expertise with the objectives of producing "great talents of virtue" who can contribute in a broad-ranging way to serving Japan and the international society.

FACULTIES

Faculty of human happiness

Students in this faculty will pursue liberal arts from various perspectives with a multidisciplinary approach, explore and envision an ideal state of human beings and society.

Faculty of successful management

This faculty aims to realize successful management that helps organizations to create value and wealth for society and to contribute to the happiness and the development of management and employees as well as society as a whole.

Faculty of future creation

Students in this faculty study subjects such as political science, journalism, performing arts and artistic expression, and explore and present new political and cultural models based on truth, goodness and beauty.

Faculty of future industry

This faculty aims to nurture engineers who can resolve various issues facing modern civilization from a technological standpoint and contribute to the creation of new industries of the future.

ABOUT IRH PRESS USA

IRH Press USA Inc. was founded in 2013 as an affiliated firm of IRH Press Co., Ltd. Based in New York, the press publishes books in various categories including spirituality, religion, and self-improvement and publishes books by Ryuho Okawa, the author of over 100 million books sold worldwide. For more information, visit okawabooks.com.

Follow us on:

f Facebook: Okawa Books   **⊙** Instagram: OkawaBooks
▶ Youtube: Okawa Books   **🐦** Twitter: Okawa Books
𝓟 Pinterest: Okawa Books   **g** Goodreads: Ryuho Okawa

——— **NEWSLETTER** ———

To receive book related news, promotions and events, please subscribe to our newsletter below.

🔗 eepurl.com/bsMeJj

——— **AUDIO / VISUAL MEDIA** ———

YOUTUBE   **PODCAST**

Introduction of Ryuho Okawa's titles; topics ranging from self-help, current affairs, spirituality, religion, and the universe.

BOOKS BY RYUHO OKAWA

RYUHO OKAWA'S LAWS SERIES

The Laws Series is an annual volume of books that are comprised of Ryuho Okawa's lectures that function as universal guidance to all people. They are of various topics that were given in accordance with the changes that each year brings. *The Laws of the Sun*, the first publication of the laws series, ranked in the annual best-selling list in Japan in 1994. Since, the laws series' titles have ranked in the annual best-selling list every year for more than two decades, setting socio-cultural trends in Japan and around the world.

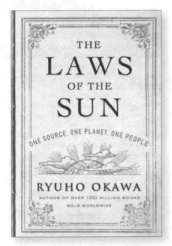

THE LAWS OF THE SUN

ONE SOURCE, ONE PLANET, ONE PEOPLE

Paperback • 288 pages • $15.95
ISBN: 978-1-942125-43-3 (Oct. 15, 2018)

IMAGINE IF YOU COULD ASK GOD why He created this world and what spiritual laws He used to shape us— and everything around us. If we could understand His designs and intentions, we could discover what our goals in life should be and whether our actions move us closer to those goals or farther away.

At a young age, a spiritual calling prompted Ryuho Okawa to outline what he innately understood to be universal truths for all humankind. In *The Laws of the Sun*, Okawa outlines these laws of the universe and provides a road map for living one's life with greater purpose and meaning. In this powerful book, Ryuho Okawa reveals the transcendent nature of consciousness and the secrets of our multidimensional universe and our place in it. By understanding the different stages of love and following the Buddhist Eightfold Path, he believes we can speed up our eternal process of development. *The Laws of the Sun* shows the way to realize true happiness—a happiness that continues from this world through the other.

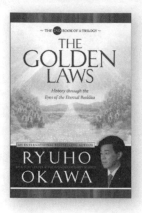

THE GOLDEN LAWS

HISTORY THROUGH THE EYES OF THE ETERNAL BUDDHA

Paperback • 201 pages • $14.95
ISBN: 978-1-941779-81-1 (Jul. 1, 2011)

Throughout history, Great Guiding Spirits have been present on Earth in both the East and the West at crucial points in human history to further our spiritual development. *The Golden Laws* reveals how Divine Plan has been unfolding on Earth, and outlines 5,000 years of the secret history of humankind. Once we understand the true course of history, through past, present and into the future, we cannot help but become aware of the significance of our spiritual mission in the present age.

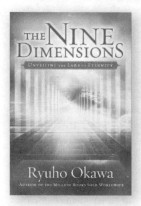

THE NINE DIMENSIONS

UNVEILING THE LAWS OF ETERNITY

Paperback • 168 pages • $15.95
ISBN: 978-0-982698-56-3 (Feb. 16, 2012)

This book is a window into the mind of our loving God, who designed this world and the vast, wondrous world of our afterlife as a school with many levels through which our souls learn and grow. When the religions and cultures of the world discover the truth of their common spiritual origin, they will be inspired to accept their differences, come together under faith in God, and build an era of harmony and peaceful progress on Earth.

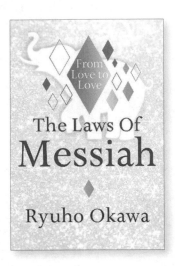

The Laws Of Messiah
From Love to Love

Paperback • 248 pages • $16.95
ISBN: 978-1-942125-90-7 (Jan. 31, 2022)

"What is Messiah?" This book carries an important message of love and guidance to people living now from the Modern-Day Messiah or the Modern-Day Savior. It also reveals the secret of Shambhala, the spiritual center of Earth, as well as the truth that this spiritual center is currently in danger of perishing and what we can do to protect this sacred place.

Love your Lord God. Know that those who don't know love don't know God. Discover the true love of God and the ideal practice of faith. This book teaches the most important element we must not lose sight of as we go through our soul training on this planet Earth.

SCHEDULED TO BE PUBLISHED IN JULY 2022

THE REBIRTH OF BUDDHA

MY ETERNAL DISCIPLES, HEAR MY WORDS

Hardcover • 256 pages • $16.95
ISBN-13: 978-1-942125-95-2

These are the messages of Buddha who has returned to this modern age as promised to His eternal beloved disciples. They are in simple words and poetic style, yet contain profound messages. Once you start reading these passages, your soul will be replenished as the plant absorbs the water, and you will remember why you chose this era to be born into with Buddha. Listen to the voices of your Eternal Master and awaken to your calling.

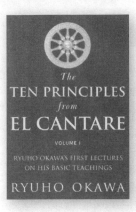

THE TEN PRINCIPLES FROM EL CANTARE VOLUME I

RYUHO OKAWA'S FIRST LECTURES ON HIS BASIC TEACHINGS

Paperback • 232 pages • $16.95
ISBN: 978-1-942125-85-3 (Dec. 15, 2021)

This book contains the historic lectures given on the first five principles of the Ten Principles of Happy Science from the author, Ryuho Okawa, who is revered as World Teacher. These lectures produced an enthusiastic fellowship in Happy Science Japan and became the foundation of the current global utopian movement. You can learn the essence of Okawa's teachings and the secret behind the rapid growth of the Happy Science movement in simple language.

NEW

THE TEN PRINCIPLES FROM EL CANTARE VOLUME II

RYUHO OKAWA'S FIRST LECTURES ON HIS WISH TO SAVE THE WORLD

Paperback • 272 pages • $16.95
ISBN: 978-1-942125-86-0 (May. 3, 2022)

A sequel to *The Ten Principles from El Cantare Volume I*. Volume II reveals the Creator's three major inventions; the secret of the creation of human souls, the meaning of time, and 'happiness' as life's purpose. By reading this book, you can not only improve yourself but learn how to make differences in society and create an ideal, utopian world.

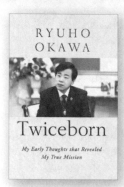

TWICEBORN

MY EARLY THOUGHTS THAT REVEALED
MY TRUE MISSION

Hardcover • 206 pages • $19.95
ISBN: 978-1-942125-74-7 (Oct. 7, 2020)

This semi-autobiography of Ryuho Okawa reveals
the origins of his thoughts and how he made up his
mind to establish Happy Science to spread the Truth
to the world. It also contains the very first grand
lecture where he declared himself as El Cantare. The
timeless wisdom in *Twiceborn* will surely inspire you
and help you fulfill your mission in this lifetime.

THE NEW RESURRECTION

MY MIRACULOUS STORY OF
OVERCOMING ILLNESS AND DEATH

Hardcover • 224 pages • $19.95
ISBN: 978-1-942125-64-8 (Feb. 26, 2020)

The New Resurrection is an autobiographical account
of an astonishing miracle experienced by author
Ryuho Okawa in 2004. This event was adapted into
the feature-length film *Immortal Hero*. Today, Okawa
lives each day with the readiness to die for the Truth
and has dedicated his life to selflessly guiding faith
seekers towards spiritual development and happiness.

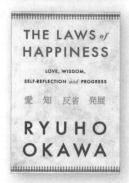

THE LAWS OF HAPPINESS

LOVE, WISDOM, SELF-REFLECTION AND PROGRESS

Paperback • 264 pages • $16.95
ISBN: 978-1-942125-70-9 (Aug. 28, 2020)

What is happiness? In this book, Ryuho Okawa
explains that happiness is not found outside us; it's
found within us, in how we think, how we look at our
lives in this world, what we believe in, and how we
devote our hearts to the work we do. Even as we go
through suffering and unfavorable circumstances, we
can always shift our mindset and become happier by
simply *giving love* instead of *taking love*.

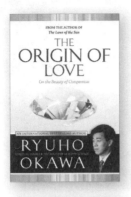

THE ORIGIN OF LOVE

ON THE BEAUTY OF COMPASSION

Paperback • 90 pages • $14.95
ISBN: 978-1-941779-83-5 (Oct. 23, 2015)

Why do people love each other, or hate each other? In this book, spiritual teacher Ryuho Okawa answers this question by referring to the origin of love in relation to the secret of eternal life. When you understand the Truth about love, you will be awakened to the wonder of being given life, and you will be filled with love for those around you.

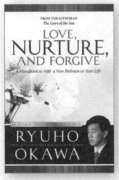

LOVE, NURTURE, AND FORGIVE

A HANDBOOK TO ADD A NEW RICHNESS TO YOUR LIFE

Paperback • 114 pages • $14.95
ISBN: 978-1-941779-75-0 (Sep. 24, 2015)

Ryuho Okawa reveals the secrets of spiritual growth based on his own real life experiences. Starting from practicing the "love that gives," instead of expecting something in return for what you have done to help others, you can experience a remarkable transformation through your own self-help efforts to develop through the stages of love.

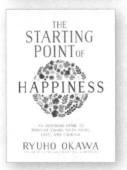

THE STARTING POINT OF HAPPINESS

AN INSPIRING GUIDE TO POSITIVE LIVING
WITH FAITH, LOVE, AND COURAGE

Paperback • 224 pages • $16.95
ISBN: 978-1-942125-26-6 (Nov. 17, 2017)

Ryuho Okawa awakens us to the true spiritual values of our life; he beautifully illustrates how we can find purpose and meaning to attain enduring happiness. Okawa empowers spiritual seekers to find the strength amidst difficult circumstances and to savor the joy of giving love to others - all in accordance with the will of the great universe. This self-renewing guide to positive living will awaken us to spiritual truths that invite authentic and lasting happiness.

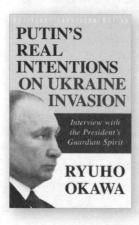

PUTIN'S REAL INTENTIONS ON UKRAINE INVASION

INTERVIEW WITH THE PRESIDENT'S GUARDIAN SPIRIT

Paperback • 216 pages • $13.95
ISBN: 978-1-943928-32-3 (Mar. 30, 2022)

Why did Russia invade Ukraine? The author and spiritual leader Ryuho Okawa conducted a spiritual interview with the guardian spirit of President Vladimir Putin in order to provide sources for the world to understand the top leader's thoughts and to make future judgements and predictions. The true nature of the Russia-Ukraine conflict and Putin's thoughts is here.

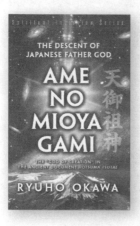

THE DESCENT OF JAPANESE FATHER GOD AME-NO-MIOYA-GAMI

THE "GOD OF CREATION" IN THE ANCIENT DOCUMENT *HOTSUMA TSUTAE*

Paperback • 276 pages • $14.95
ISBN: 978-1-943928-29-3 (Feb. 12, 2022)

By reading this book, you can find the origin of bushido (samurai spirit) and understand how the ancient Japanese civilization influenced other countries. Now that the world is in confusion, Japan is expected to awaken to its true origin and courageously rise to bring justice to the world.

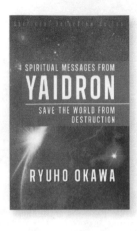

SPIRITUAL MESSAGES FROM YAIDRON SAVE THE WORLD FROM DESTRUCTION

Paperback • 190 pages • $11.95
ISBN: 978-1-943928-23-1 (Dec. 25, 2021)

In this book, Yaidron explains what was going on behind the military coup in Myanmar and Taliban's control over Afghanistan. He also warns of the imminent danger approaching Taiwan. According to what he observes from the universe, World War III has already begun on Earth. What is now going on is a battle between democratic values and the communist one-party control. How to overcome this battle and create peace on Earth depends on the faith and righteous actions of each one of us.

SPIRITUAL MESSAGES FROM METATRON LIGHT IN THE TIMES OF CRISIS

Paperback • 146 pages • $11.95
ISBN: 978-1-943928-19-4 (Nov. 4, 2021)

Metatron is one of the highest-ranking angels (seraphim) in Judaism and Christianity, and also one of the saviors of universe who has guided the civilizations of many planets including Earth, under the guidance of Lord God. Such savior has sent a message upon seeing the crisis of Earth. You will also learn about the truth behind the coronavirus pandemic, the unimaginable extent of China's desire, the danger of appeasement policy toward China, and the secret of Metatron.

THE LAWS OF SECRET
Awaken to This New World and Change Your Life

THE LAWS OF FAITH
One World Beyond Differences

THE LAWS OF MISSION
Essential Truths for Spiritual Awakening in a Secular Age

THE HELL YOU NEVER KNEW
And How to Avoid Going There

THE REAL EXORCIST
Attain Wisdom to Conquer Evil

SPIRITUAL WORLD 101
A Guide to a Spiritually Happy Life

THE POSSESSION
Know the Ghost Condition and Overcome
Negative Spiritual Influence

THE AGE OF MERCY
Overcoming Religious Conflicts under
the Supreme God, El Cantare

LOVE FOR THE FUTURE
Building One World of Freedom and Democracy
Under God's Truth

For a complete list of books, visit <u>okawabooks.com</u>